A WOMAN'S HEART *for* GOD

Drawing Closer to the Lover of Your Soul

SHEILA CRAGG

WORTHY
PUBLISHING

Published by Worthy Publishing, a division of Worthy Media, Inc., 134 Franklin Road, Suite 200, Brentwood, Tennessee 37027.

HELPING PEOPLE EXPERIENCE THE HEART OF GOD
eBook available at www.worthypublishing.com

Library of Congress Control Number: 2012956457

Portions of this book were adapted from Sheila Cragg's previous books *A Woman's Walk with God* and *Journey toward Holiness*.

Unless otherwise noted, Scripture quotations are taken from Holy Bible, New International Version®, NIV® Copyright © 1973, 1978, 1984 by Biblica, Inc.® Used by permission. All rights reserved worldwide.

Scripture quotations marked differently are as follows: AMP are taken from The Amplified Bible: Old Testament. ©1962, 1964 by Zondervan (used by permission); and from The Amplified Bible: New Testament. © 1958 by the Lockman Foundation (used by permission). ESV are taken from The English Standard Version. © 2001 by Crossway Bibles, a division of Good News Publishers. KJV are taken from KING JAMES VERSION. MSG are taken from The Message by Eugene H. Peterson. © 1993, 1994, 1995, 1996, 2000, 2001, 2002. Used by permission of NavPress Publishing Group. All rights reserved. NIV2011 are taken from Holy Bible, New International Version®, NIV® Copyright © 1973, 1978, 1984, 2011 by Biblica, Inc.® Used by permission. All rights reserved worldwide. NKJV are taken from The Holy Bible, New King James Version Copyright © 1982 by Thomas Nelson, Inc. NLT1996 are taken from Holy Bible. New Living Translation copyright© 1996 by Tyndale House Foundation. Used by permission of Tyndale House Publishers Inc., Carol Stream, Illinois 60188. All rights reserved. NLT2007 are taken from Holy Bible. New Living Translation copyright© 1996, 2004, 2007 by Tyndale House Foundation. Used by permission of Tyndale House Publishers Inc., Carol Stream, Illinois 60188. All rights reserved. PHILLIPS are taken from J. B. Phillips: The New Testament In Modern English, Revised Edition. © J. B. Phillips 1958, 1960, 1972. Used by permission of Macmillan Publishing Co., Inc. RSV are taken from Revised Standard Version of the Bible. © 1946, 1952, 1971, 1973 by the Division of Christian Education of the National Council of the Churches of Christ in the U.S.A. Used by permission. TNIV are taken from Holy Bible, Today's New International Version® TNIV® Copyright © 2001, 2005 by Biblica®. All rights reserved worldwide. GW are taken from GOD'S WORD, © 1995 God's Word to the Nations. Used by permission of Baker Publishing Group.

For foreign and subsidiary rights, contact Riggins International Rights Services, Inc., www.rigginsrights.com

ISBN: 978-1-61795-159-6

Cover Design: Faceout Studio
Cover Image: ©Veer and Visual Photos
Interior Typesetting: Susan Browne Design

Printed in the United States of America

13 14 15 16 17 QGFF 8 7 6 5 4 3 2 1

To my faithful friends:

Edith Hintz, Barbara York, Christine McNeil,
and Nancy Landahl

CONTENTS

PART FIVE: THE SERVANT LIFE

ACKNOWLEDGMENTS

God has amazing ways of bringing people together. I call those encounters "divine appointments," and that is how this book was born.

I was searching for Christian publishers on the Internet when I came across Kris Bearss, executive editor at Worthy Publishing. I knew her from her work on three of my earlier books, but we had not been in contact for years. I called her and was warmly received. *A Woman's Heart for God* is the result of that divine appointment. A special thanks to Kris and also to Byron Williamson, the president of Worthy, and all the Worthy staff for believing in this book.

Elisa Fryling Stanford was my main editor, and I could not have completed this book without her. She is kind and gracious, gifted and insightful, helpful and supportive. She is a wonderful encourager. She has revised and rearranged and rewritten large portions of this book. Thank you ever so much!

A special thank you to senior editor, Jennifer Day, and to copy editor, Lisa Guest. Their insights, revisions, and suggestions were perceptive and welcomed.

I am so grateful to Kyle Olund of KLO Publishing Service for guiding me through the proofreading and publishing process and to Morgan Canclini and Alyson White in publicity and marketing for all their work in publicizing this book.

FOREWORD

Sometimes life can fall apart. That certainly seems to be Naomi's experience in the book of Ruth—and the tragedies in her life get collapsed into just five verses! By the time you finish reading Ruth 1:1-5, you've encountered one famine, one major relocation, two marriages, and three funerals—and you're left with three widows. Sometimes life can fall apart in just a few verses. At the time of this writing, I am preaching through the book of Ruth at the church where I serve as pastor. We've experienced a great deal of suffering in our church body lately, a great deal of Ruth 1:1-5 loss and pain.

As I've studied God's message in this wonderful Old Testament book, I've grown fond of Naomi. She is a widow living in patriarchal Israel when women were dependent upon men for survival, and it's the time of the judges when "everyone did what was right in his own eyes" (Judges 21:25 ESV). I feel for Naomi: her faith is wavering, and she is doubting God. Naomi's great mistake is that she is letting her pain paint her picture of God.

What would you say to Naomi? If I could hop in a time machine and go back in time, I'd do my best to offer her pastoral counsel. I'd do my best to reassure her that God is good. I'd pray for her. And if I could give her a book to read, I'd give her the book that you're holding in your hand. Whether Sheila Cragg realizes it or not, she has written a book for Naomi.

A Woman's Heart for God: Drawing Closer to the Lover of Your Soul is exactly what Naomi needed. She, like many women (and men!), had lost sight of that great gospel promise that God loves us more than we could ever imagine or dream. But I think that if Naomi had a copy of this book, she would feel her heart moving once again toward the Lover of her soul.

I'm happy to recommend Sheila's book to you. The first thing that you need to know about *A Woman's Heart for God* is that this book is God-centered—and isn't that what you're looking for in a book? Sheila repeatedly returns to the gospel, the Good News, that God loves His children not because of what they do for Him, but because of what His Son, Jesus, has done for them.

This book will continually remind you of the life, death, and resurrection of Jesus. This book is the perfect marriage of passion and practicality. And this book is a peek into the heart of one woman's honest, real, and raw struggle to love Jesus as she experienced what Paul calls "light momentary affliction":

"We do not lose heart. Though our outer self is wasting away, our inner self is being renewed day by day. For this light momentary affliction is preparing for us an eternal weight of glory beyond all comparison, as we look not to the things that are seen but to the things that are unseen. For the things that are seen are transient, but the things that are unseen are eternal." (2 Corinthians 4:16-18 ESV)

Sheila will help you see that though outwardly you may be wasting away, you can be renewed inwardly each day. She will help you again see Jesus as the Great Redeemer of every sorrow and pain you have experienced.

As I read *A Woman's Heart for God*, I kept thinking, "Yes! I have been there and felt like that. I can relate to that struggle. I'm not the only one who struggles like that!" Reading this book was like meeting a friend at Starbucks for coffee and conversation. As you read, I think you'll feel as if Sheila is sitting across the table from you, talking with you, not at you.

Whether or not you feel like Naomi right now, this book will help you center your affections once again on Jesus, the Lover of your soul. So go ahead and grab a cup of coffee. Find a nice place to sit and get cozy. My friend Sheila wants to tell you about her Friend.

Benji Magness
Senior Pastor
Grace Baptist Church
Santa Maria, California

INTRODUCTION

I am certain that God, who began the good work within you,
will continue his work until it is finally finished
on the day when Christ Jesus returns.

—*Philippians 1:6* NLT

I used to think it was all up to me. My relationship with God. My commitment to spiritual disciplines. Even whether or not things were going "right" in my life.

I used to believe that the way to a deeper relationship with God was to have personal objectives that I worked toward every day. I set monthly, yearly, and lifelong goals and tried to develop habits that I believed would help me grow in my relationship with God.

I even wrote three devotional Bible studies based on my own spiritual strivings. Here is what I wrote in a book years ago: "God is gracious, patient, and tender, but He desires our utmost for His highest. It requires constant work to maintain the disciplines."

I was basing everything on *my* efforts, *my* plans, *my* determination to please God with *my* devotional life. All well-meaning, but it was all self-driven, not God-driven. It was based on my working to get closer to God rather than daily waiting on His guidance and listening for what He wanted to teach me during my time with Him.

And I kept failing! Instead of helping me, the goals I set for myself made me feel like a disappointment to God when I didn't achieve them or even work toward them. Those goals kept me from resting in the Lord.

Then, soon after my third devotional Bible study was published, my life fell apart. I'll give you more details in the chapter called "Being Crucified with Christ," but between health and family struggles, nothing seemed to be going right. Most significantly, for six and a half years, my family fought for custody rights of my son's foster children.

I begged God to answer prayers and deliver us from our trials. Yet for all those years, God didn't answer my prayers my way or in my timing. Instead, He taught me to watch for Him working in our trials, in the unchanging circumstances. As a result, I saw His work in many places I would have missed, and I drew closer to Him instead of feeling alienated from Him.

God used that very difficult ten-year period—and He is using the struggles that continue even now—to teach me that He is sovereign. He is the Chooser, the Planner, the Director. My deeper relationship with God is up to Him, not me: He will guide me and instruct me in His ways.

God also taught me to fight for the rights of my son and daughter-in-law's foster daughters—for the girls' protection—through prayer as well as through pleading with those in authority. I tell you that because I want to emphasize that leading a God-directed life does not mean that we do nothing. It means we fight for what is right, we actively respond to God's call, we seek more knowledge of our divine Lover—while at the same time submitting to Him and watching for Him to work.

In other words, my first books were a lot about what I must do for God. This book is about how I respond to God and how He wants me to serve Him and others. You and I can make plans for our spiritual life, but God designs it. Our job is to respond with obedience and joy to what God does.

So what does that paradox of God's initiative and our action look like? In *A Woman's Heart for God*, we'll look at steps we can take as God guides us on our spiritual journey. We'll also see why God is the initiator in our relationship with Him. Our spiritual life begins with God, and the Holy Spirit helps us sustain our faith.

Once you understand that truth in your heart as well as your mind, you will be freed to enjoy God and glorify His name, you will be freed to watch Him work according to His plans and purposes for your life, and you will be freed to receive—even in your darkest hours—the deep peace that can only come from Him.

Why? Because we are freest when we are leading God-directed lives. We are freest when we submit to the life God has chosen for us, as we watch for Him to work in us despite painful circumstances that stay the same.

Each chapter in this book ends with a prayer based on Scripture. I invite you to read those prayers slowly and to stop when a particular word or phrase resonates with you. Then ask God what He might want to show you through those words.

After each of those prayers, you'll find several questions for reflection. If you are going through this book with a prayer partner or a group, you may want to talk about the questions together. Whether you are reading alone or with someone else, you may want to journal your answers or use them as springboards to prayer.

As you read, remember that we cannot possibly become committed to God or lead a disciplined life or form healthy spiritual habits by our personal efforts. We will fail every time.

Developing good spiritual habits means surrendering to the God-directed life. It means listening to the Holy Spirit direct you in this season of life—whether it's an exhausting season with young children demanding your time, an intense season of finding your place in your vocation, or a lonely season of waiting and reflecting.

Only God's power can help us develop the disciplined life, and that process takes a lifetime. I'm still traveling on this spiritual road. In recent years I've been in a long period of questioning that has left me with no answers this side of heaven. My life sometimes feels like an unfinished puzzle with pieces scattered all over the table, pieces that only God can put together.

The more I submit to what the Lord wants of me, the more God-given peace I experience even in the midst of pain. The more I see the joy of not knowing the answers but of instead developing a deeper heart for God. I'm learning, as I go, the beauty of resting in my relationship with Him and the joy of knowing Him, not just knowing about Him.

This is the relationship of two who love each other. As we read in Song of Songs, "This is my beloved and this is my friend" (Song of Songs 5:16 ESV). This is the relationship God wants each of us to have with Him as we respond to His great love.

Let's continue the journey together.

Part One

THE

GOD-CENTERED

LIFE

CHAPTER 1

LONGING
FOR GOD

It is the LORD your God you must follow,
and him you must revere.
Keep his commands and obey him;
serve him and hold fast to him.

—Deuteronomy 13:4, TNIV

My homesickness surprised me. We had anticipated moving to Santa Maria for such a long time, and now we were living close to our sons and their families. I loved my new home, but I felt a restless longing to return to Orange County where we had lived for most of our married life.

One weekend I went back for a visit. It eased my homesickness to drive through our neighborhood and see family, friends, and familiar places. When I went to our old house to pick up mail, the Hispanic family living there warmly welcomed me and insisted on giving me a tour. It was the first house they had ever bought. As the mother took me through every room, I saw how pleased she was to have her own home.

The father had been a migrant worker and was now a ranch fore-man. As Andre, their grown son, showed me how his father had turned the yard into a fruit orchard and garden, he proudly named every tree and vegetable. I left with a bag of luscious, homegrown tomatoes and an overflowing heart. I was delighted that this gracious family was living in our old house.

For many years, I was an English as a Second Language teacher. I taught hundreds of migrant workers English, and though most lived in poverty, they were always so generous and appreciative. This family's warm ways and words of heartfelt gratitude brought to mind the hundreds of students whose kindnesses had touched my life through the years.

KNOWING GOD

God not only created us to be homesick for loved ones and home but also homesick for Himself and heaven. As St. Augustine put it, "You have made us for yourself, and our heart is restless until it rests in you."[1]

As we grow in our desire to become a woman who has a heart for God, we find ourselves wanting to know Him more. Who is this God who has pursued, wooed, and won us? This Lover of our soul—what is He like?

As the *Westminster Confession* states: "There is but one only living and true God, who is infinite in being and perfection, a most pure spirit . . . immutable, immense, eternal . . . almighty, most wise, most holy, most free, most absolute . . . most loving, gracious, merciful, long-suffering, abundant in goodness and truth, forgiving iniquity, transgression and sin; the rewarder of them that diligently seek him."[2]

The Lord our God is one God, but He relates to us in different capacities.

He is the Creator of the universe, our Father and Provider, who meets all of our needs.

He is Jesus, our Savior, who identified with us by coming to us in human flesh and demonstrating His healing compassion and love. He understands and cares about our earthly concerns, needs, and problems. He is our Redeemer, and through Him we have eternal life.

He is also the Holy Spirit, who convicts us and delivers us from sin. He indwells us, is ever-present, ever-caring, and meets our deepest heart cries, which no other human being can do for us. He is our Comforter and Counselor who guides us. The Holy Spirit empowers us to serve the Lord and enables us to use our spiritual gifts.

A. W. Tozer said this about the mystery of the Trinity: "God is in complete harmony and agreement with Himself. His justice does not contradict His mercy; His judgment of the lost does not contradict His forgiveness and grace to the redeemed."[3]

God does not distance Himself from us. To the contrary, He wants us to know Him, and growing in our knowledge of Him comprises our spiritual journey. It amazes me that the God who created the universe and everything in it wants me to know Him on a personal level!

Let's look more closely at this amazing God who longs to be in relationship with us and meet our every need.

GOD IS LOVING

Our greatest human need is to experience love. Hear how A. W. Tozer described that love: "Because God is self-sufficient, His love had no beginning; because He is eternal, His love can have no end; because He is infinite, it has no limit . . . because He is immense, His love is an incomprehensibly vast, bottomless, shoreless sea before which we kneel in joyful silence."[4]

Occasionally I have caught a glimpse of godly love in Christian couples who have been married for many years. They have a oneness and tender affection that is inspiring. Though they have experienced numerous hardships together, those adversities strengthened their commitment and devotion to the Lord and to each other.

Just as those husbands and wives pledged their loyalty to God and to each other, we can vow our love and faithfulness to our most Beloved. We can choose to believe in the depths of our hearts that God loves us with a holy love as passionately as a groom loves his bride. Furthermore, Jesus is an ever-faithful Husband.

As our love for Him grows stronger over time, as we remain spiritually steadfast in adversity, we will develop a deeper fellowship with Him and a greater assurance of His love.

Again, we may feel distant from God when we experience trouble. But God's very nature is love, so He cannot withhold His love from us. No matter what hardships we experience, God loves us. He has not forsaken us, and He never will.

The apostle Paul's declaration can be yours and mine: "I am convinced that neither death nor life, neither angels nor demons, neither the present nor the future, nor any powers, neither height nor depth, nor anything else in all creation, will be able to separate us from the love of God that is in Christ Jesus our Lord" (Romans 8:38-39).

GOD IS HOLY

God is holy and untouched by sin. God is holy, pure, and infinite in His perfection. Any defect in God's character would mean that He is imperfect, which He can never be.

We can rest with absolute security in His love and His holiness. "For I will proclaim the name of the Lord; ascribe greatness to our God! 'The Rock, his work is perfect, for all his ways are justice. A God of faithfulness and without iniquity, just and upright is he" (Deuteronomy 32:3–4 ESV). As Tozer wrote, "Holy is the way God is. To be holy, He does not conform to a standard. He is that standard. He is absolutely holy with an infinite, incomprehensible fullness of purity that is incapable of being other than it is. Because He is holy, His attributes are holy."[5]

It was this holy God who sent His Son to die on the cross so that we might share in His holiness. The best-known verse of Scripture makes that fact very clear: "For God so loved the world, that he gave his only begotten Son, that whosoever believeth in him should not perish, but have everlasting life. For God sent not his Son into the world to condemn the world; but that the world through him might be saved" (John 3:16-17 KJV).

Consider the evidence of how important holiness is to our pure and righteous God: "He loves righteousness in the life of His children to such a degree that He gave His only begotten Son to secure it. The Cross shows how much God loves holiness. The Cross stands for God's holiness before even His love. For Christ died not merely for our sins, but in order that He might provide us with that righteousness of life which God loves."[6]

GOD IS ALWAYS THE SAME

We need the assurance that God does not change. The owner of a large company I once worked for did not trust his employees, and his mistrust made him such a changeable and inconsistent leader that we could not figure out what pleased him and what displeased him. Not only did we feel insecure, but we wasted a great deal of energy and company time trying to meet his unpredictable and poorly defined expectations.

In sharp contrast, I taught at a college where my supervisors were consistent and reliable, and they clearly communicated their expectations. They also constantly expressed their confidence and trust in their staff.

The result of their consistency and encouragement? We were far more committed and productive because we felt appreciated and secure—and we gladly worked overtime!

In the same way, we can rely on God to be consistent, reliable, and unchangeable in His expectations of us. We know, for instance, that "Jesus Christ is the same yesterday and today and forever" (Hebrews 13:8), so the standards do not and will not change.

God is who He says He is, and He always will be. God's ways are what He says they are, and they always will be. What God has promised He will perform. He can never be unfaithful or unloving because that would require the impossible: for Him to change.

But since we humans constantly change and contradict ourselves, we find it difficult to conceive of Someone who doesn't. One reason we are changeable people is because God Himself gave us the power to think and act and choose as we please. This free will—this freedom to change for good or bad—may seem a curse, because the sins we humans commit result in so much suffering. But this freedom to change is in reality a blessing.

Tozer spoke to this truth: "In a fallen world such as this, the very ability to change is a golden treasure, a gift from God of such fabulous worth as to call for constant thanksgiving. For human beings the whole possibility of redemption lies in the ability to change. To move across from one sort of person to another is the essence of repentance: the liar becomes truthful, the thief honest, the lewd pure, the proud humble. The whole moral texture of the life is altered. The thoughts, the desires, the affections are transformed."[7]

GOD IS MERCIFUL AND LONG-SUFFERING

We are blessed to know that God is merciful and patient. We find that truth proclaimed throughout the Bible. For instance, Paul wrote this: "When the kindness and love of God our Savior appeared, he saved us, not because of righteous things we had done, but because of his mercy" (Titus 3:4-5). Jesus Himself demonstrated the compassionate mercy of God in His ministry here on earth, and that mercy is infinite and inexhaustible.

God is also long-suffering: He is slow to anger, and He demonstrates patience and self-restraint in the face of provocation by sinful, ungrateful human beings. The apostle Peter said, "The Lord does not delay and is not tardy or slow about what He promises, according to some people's conception of slowness, but He is long-suffering (extraordinarily patient) toward you, not desiring that any should perish, but that all should turn to repentance" (2 Peter 3:9 AMP).

Though we may often fall and wonder if we will ever overcome our habitual sins, God is ready to forgive (Psalm 86:5). We are to pray boldly for God's help for all our needs, sins, and weaknesses (Hebrews 4:16), for He is willing to deliver us from sin and give us the strength we need to change.

GOD IS EVER-PRESENT

We need to experience God's constant and abiding presence with us. We desire closeness in human relationships, but no one can be with us at all times the way God is. He watches over us and is with us wherever we go. He sees everything we do and knows our every thought. He knows everything that happens to us, both good and evil.

We may feel alone and abandoned by God, however, when we are going through tough times, our life is in turmoil, and trials grow worse. We cannot feel His presence, and as we focus on our expectations of what God should do and lock into how He should solve our heartaches, we can become more and more convinced that He does not care and is not present with us. Once we relinquish our expectations and demands of how God should answer, we are then freed to experience His presence in our lives and to see how He has been working in the background all along.

We can be assured that the Lord our Shepherd will guide us through life's darkest valleys, deepest rivers, and most fiery trials. His thoughts of us are precious and so constant we cannot count them, for they number far more than all the grains of sand in the world (Psalm 139; Isaiah 43:2).

What great comfort to know that our Sovereign God is constantly watching over us and listening to us. If we are Christians, His Spirit dwells within us. No one is as close to us as the Spirit of God, and no one cares more about us than He does. He is with us, within us, and will be with us always (Matthew 28:20).

GOD IS FAITHFUL

We have a deep need to know God's faithfulness to us. One of the deepest hurts we may experience is the wound of a loved one's unfaithfulness. And once we have been betrayed, we find it difficult to trust again—but we need to remember that we can rely on God's faithfulness even when human beings fail us. Moses offered this reassurance: "Know therefore that the LORD your God is God; he is the faithful God, keeping his covenant of love to a thousand generations of those who love him and keep his commands" (Deuteronomy 7:9).

God's faithfulness is the foundation of our eternal relationship with Him: "Upon God's faithfulness rests our whole hope of future blessedness. Only as He is faithful will His covenants stand and His promises be honored. Only as we have complete assurance that He is faithful may we live in peace and look forward with assurance to the life to come."[8]

GOD IS OUR REWARDER

God will reward us for remaining faithful to Him. As the writer to the Hebrews acknowledged, "Without faith it is impossible to please him: for he that cometh to God must believe that he is, and that he is a rewarder of them that diligently seek him" (Hebrews 11:6 KJV).

When we walk by faith and continually seek God's guidance, then no matter what difficulties we may experience, we can be confident that He will reward us for trusting Him. We will be commended for our faith even if we do not see some of our most God-honoring requests answered.

GOD IS ETERNAL

We will live forever with God. Monuments, pyramids, and statues have been erected as eternal memorials to kings, queens, presidents, movies, and sports stars. Though the world tries to preserve their legacy, they will all be forgotten (Ecclesiastes 1:11). So rather than revering human heroes past and present, let us exalt our eternal God.

King Solomon recognized the value of doing so: "Everything God does will endure forever; nothing can be added to it and nothing taken from it. God does it so that men will revere him" (Ecclesiastes 3:14).

But what if earth were all there is? Millions of us have had difficult and pain-filled lives, knowing extreme poverty, or suffering from crippling disabilities. But we can find great comfort in the thought of living forever with God without pain, and we can cling to that hope here on earth when our lives are miserable. We have an eternal future that is absolutely glorious.

Speaking of things eternal, although we are bound by time here on earth, we are actually living in eternity even now. In other words, today is part of the forever that started an immeasurably long, long time ago.

So let us lift our eyes to the heavens and praise and worship our Lord God, who is from everlasting to everlasting. For God has planned something far better for us than what this earth holds (Hebrews 11:39-40). Jesus is preparing a place for us, an eternal home in heaven where we will enjoy the rewards of dwelling forever with Him (John 14:2-3).

⌒

Knowing God and His holy attributes provides a solid and unshakable foundation for our spiritual life. Knowing God means resting in the promise that "he who began a good work in you will bring it to completion at the day of Jesus Christ" (Philippians 1:6 ESV). And knowing God gives us the assurance we need to trust Him with our lives and to grow in our faith in all circumstances.

This kind of knowing with our head, however needs to be undergirded by our knowing God in our heart, especially knowing that He loves us. As you read chapter 2, may you hear in your heart the truths that proclaim God's great love for you.

↭ *Prayer* ↭

Sovereign Lord, the One who never changes, Your plans "stand firm forever, the purposes of [Your] heart through all generations" . . . "In the beginning you laid the foundations of the earth, and the heavens are the work of your hands. They will perish, but you remain; they will all wear out like a garment. Like clothing you will change them and they will be discarded. But you remain the same, and your years will never end." . . . Yes, Jesus, Your name is called Wonderful Counselor, Mighty God, Everlasting Father, Prince of Peace . . . Above all, You are love.

—PSALM 33:11; PSALM 102:25–27; ISAIAH 9:6–7; 1 JOHN 4:8

↭ *Practicing the Spiritual Life* ↭

1. Which attributes of God do you most appreciate today? Why?

2. What attribute of God is the hardest for you to understand? Why?

3. What is your deepest need right now? Which attribute(s) of God meet that need?

4. For what situations in your life do you most need reassurance that God never changes?

CHAPTER 2

CONFIDENT IN GOD'S LOVE

Love the LORD your God
with all your heart
and with all your soul
and with all your strength.

—*Deuteronomy 6:5*

When I was in sixth grade, the nurse weighed and measured all the kids in my school. As I stepped up to the scale, I could see the other children's measurements. Though I was one of the youngest in my class, I was the tallest child—five feet, six inches—in the entire school. On top of that, I had become heavy in the sixth grade, and only one boy weighed more than I did.

The boys teased me, calling me "Sheila Monster" and "Gila Monster."

When I told my mother, she said, "Kids only tease the people they like."

I couldn't buy that one at all. In fact, her reply further diminished my feelings of self-worth.

I also had large, flat feet, and my best friend's dad teased me, saying, "Here comes tugboat feet."

My stepfather was verbally cruel to all of us—to his two daughters as well as to my brother and me. We couldn't say anything without being corrected. We were always wrong, and our opinions were worthless. And he continued to treat us that way even when we became adults.

By seventh grade, I was slender, and I stayed that way into young adulthood. But no matter how slender I looked or how well I did in school or what I achieved, I never felt good about myself or my appearance.

In addition, I was not raised in a Christian home. Our family rarely went to church, so I did not hear the gospel until I was sixteen and accepted Jesus as my Savior. I didn't know anything about the Bible, so I felt like I was at a disadvantage compared to others my age who had strong Christian backgrounds.

It's no surprise, then, that I have often questioned why God would want to use me to write books about the spiritual life. I often feel utterly unworthy of this calling. I constantly struggle not to give in to my feeling inferior, not to give up, and not to stop doing what God has called me to do. Sadly, my self-criticism has hindered me from doing His will on many occasions.

Do you find that feeling bad about yourself sometimes keeps you from approaching God? Do feelings of shame or inferiority hold you back from believing God loves you and has specific plans for you to serve Him, plans that will be good for you and will bring glory to Him?

The Old Testament example of King David gives us hope that God calls imperfect people—even those whom others believe are insignificant—to serve Him.

SCENE I: THE FORGOTTEN SON

In 1 Samuel 16, we learn that Saul reigned over Israel, but when King Saul sinned against the Lord, the Almighty directed Samuel the priest to anoint another king in Saul's place.

So, as directed by the Lord, Samuel went to Bethlehem. His visit was an extremely important occasion for that small town. After all, Samuel was the chief judge and prophet over Israel, so his unexpected arrival was like having the chief justice of the United States Supreme Court come to your town. In our day, choosing and anointing a new king would draw international TV coverage.

When Samuel arrived in Bethlehem, the city elders—trembling with fear—met him. Assuring them he had come in peace, he ordered the elders to consecrate themselves and then attend the sacrifice he had planned. After issuing those instructions, Samuel consecrated a man named Jesse and his sons and then invited them to the sacrifice as well.

Once they all came together, Samuel saw Eliab, the oldest son of Jesse, and thought he was the Lord's chosen king.

But the prophet was wrong. "The LORD said to Samuel, 'Do not look on his appearance or on the height of his stature, because I have rejected him. For the LORD sees not as man sees: man looks on the outward appearance, but the LORD looks on the heart'" (1 Samuel 16:7 ESV).

Jesse had seven of his sons pass before Samuel, but the Lord told Samuel He had not chosen any of them. When Samuel asked if there were any more sons, Jesse said there was one more, the youngest. Jesse didn't even mention his son by name, implying that David was not worthy or qualified. After all, he was the youngest, and he was doing the despised job of tending sheep.

But the moment Samuel saw David, the Lord instructed him to take a horn of oil and anoint David, which the prophet did in front of David's brothers.

SCENE II: THE FORGOTTEN KING

At that time, Israel was at war, and Jesse's three oldest sons had followed Saul into battle. David, the newly anointed king of Israel, was functioning as an errand boy for his father, taking food to his brothers at the front lines, checking on how they were doing, reporting back to Jesse, and then returning to the sheep.

When David got to the battlefield, he learned that for forty days, the giant Goliath had come out and taunted King Saul and the army of Israel, daring one of the soldiers to fight him. While he was there, David heard the challenge and asked one of the men what would be done for the man who killed Goliath.

At that, David's oldest brother Eliab, who had not been chosen as king, responded angrily. He called David "proud and wicked at heart," accused him of coming to the battlefront just to watch the show, and rudely reminded him that he was only a lowly shepherd (1 Samuel 17:28).

David could have retaliated with "Who do you think you are, big brother? God didn't choose you. Samuel anointed me, not you, and I'm the next king of Israel!" But instead David simply replied, "Now what have I done? . . . Can't I even speak?" (1 Samuel 17:29).

Have you ever been treated unfairly the way David was? Can you imagine how David felt—and have you felt like that?

I am amazed by David's tenacity in the face of such wrongful treatment and his brother's harassment. Yet, despite this opposition, David was determined to do what God desired. So he went to Saul and said he would slay Goliath, which David did with his slingshot and a single stone.

Later, speaking through the apostle Paul in Acts 13:22, God said this: "I have found David son of Jesse a man after my own heart; he will do everything I want him to do."

David stood strong as a man with a heart for God because he focused his attention not on the words or opinions of others but on the living God Himself.

David silenced his accusers by doing exactly what God wanted him to do, pointing the people around him to God, and giving God all the credit and glory.

David knew that his worth in God's eyes was not dependent on how others viewed him. He stood strong in God's view of him, confident in God's calling, God's plan, God's love. David's example here is key for us as we become women after God's own heart.

A HEART FOR GOD

We will never believe that we are women after God's own heart until we realize our worth in His eyes and choose to live according to His values and His commands. But how do we come to the point of being able to say, *No matter how inferior and unworthy I feel, no matter how difficult my life, no matter what others think about me or my appearance, I can be absolutely confident that God loves me?*

In other words, how do we draw closer to the Lover of our soul so we can be confident of His love for us no matter what message our circumstances and relationships tell us?

1. We need to realize the depth and breadth of God's love for us.

Ephesians 3:17–19 (NLT 1996) says this: "I pray that Christ will be more and more at home in your hearts as you trust in him. May your roots go down deep into the soil of God's marvelous love. And may you have the power to understand, as all God's people should, how wide, how long, how high, and how deep his love really is. May you experience the love of Christ, though it is so great you will never fully understand it. Then you will be filled with the fullness of life and power that comes from God."

The more clearly we realize that Christ is "at home in [our] hearts," the more fully we are able to trust Him and the deeper our roots of faith can go down into "the soil of [His] marvelous love."

We understand that we cannot earn God's love, but feelings of inferiority keep us from receiving it. All we can think about is what we need to change about ourselves before He can love us.

Moreover, when we don't like ourselves, we are quicker to judge others. But when we open our hearts to God and accept ourselves as God's beloved, we have more grace with which to love others. When we are convinced that we have worth in God's sight, we are better able to appreciate other people's worth in God's sight.

Christ's love for us has nothing to do with our flaws, faults, frailties, outward appearance, or the opinions of others. It has little to do with us at all, in fact, and a lot more to do with God. Psalm 48:9 tells us to meditate on God's unfailing love because God's love draws us first to Him. When we meditate on God's love, we are storing in our hearts a little bit more of the truth of just "how wide, how long, how high, and how deep his love [for us] is" (Ephesians 3:18 NLT).

2. We need to remember that every person God greatly uses, He greatly humbles.

We see this pattern throughout the Bible, so may we remember that God can use even the lowest times of our life to prepare us to serve Him. After all, He used the skills David developed as a shepherd to slay the giant Goliath.

During a particularly dark time in my life, I spent most of my days feeling angry, overwhelmed, and deeply sad. My husband had recently gone blind. I was desperate to earn income to support our family, but everything I tried failed. I didn't make enough in my part-time jobs to pay the mounting medical bills and other expenses. I didn't know what to do.

Finally, when our savings and retirement funds were gone and our debts were greater than we could pay in our lifetime, we had to declare bankruptcy. It was a season of great humility. I felt defeated, and I wondered, *Why hasn't God helped me earn enough income?*

As I look back now, I see how those experiences were not enemies but were instead actually gifts from God. Humbling seasons remind us yet again that we are not God. On a more positive note, nothing can prevent the Lord from accomplishing His good purpose for our lives even when things make no sense to us and turn out much different than we had prayed for.

During those difficult years, I often came across this verse in conversation or my reading: "Be still, and know that I am God" (Psalm 46:10 KJV). God was teaching me that He is God and I am not and that, rather than striving to solve my family's problems, I needed to be still. I needed to watch for Him. I needed to listen. I needed to declare bankruptcy even though it was something I'd never imagined doing. Even though it seemed so wrong!

But Christ's power is magnified in our weakness. If we find our identity in being God's beloved, we can stop letting our addiction to perfection consume us. If we find our identity in being God's beloved, we will bring glory to Him in our weaknesses and point others to Him.

3. We need to realize that our worth in God's eyes is not based on how others view us.

God knows our character and our gifts (even ones we don't recognize yet), and He knows what He desires to do in our lives. He also knows our hearts. If He wants to use us to serve and glorify Him, He will do so no matter what others think of us or even what we think of ourselves. To become a woman with a heart for God, we need to embrace God's heart for us.

In Matthew 10:28-31, Jesus said that we're not to "be afraid of those who kill the body but cannot kill the soul. Rather, be afraid of the One who can destroy both soul and body in hell." Jesus went on to say that sparrows are only worth two cents, but God knows when even a sparrow falls to the ground. We human beings are worth more than many sparrows. In fact, we have so much worth in God's eyes that He numbers the very hairs on our head.

4. We need to respond to God's invitation to develop spiritual beauty.

In 1 Peter 3:4 we read, "You should be known for the beauty that comes from within, the unfading beauty of a gentle and quiet spirit, which is so precious to God" (NLT1996). Think of the people you know who have this kind of inner spiritual beauty. They are "steadfast, immovable, always abounding in the work of the Lord" (1 Corinthians 15:58 ESV). They are among God's beloved, but are they perfect in their outward appearance? Are they perfect Christians in every way? In a word, no.

But when I think of women who love the Lord and who serve Him and others faithfully, I think little of their outward appearance. The amazing thing is that when a woman has the confidence that comes from knowing God's love for her, she radiates His beauty. Her outward appearance pales next to the glory of God's light shining in her and through her.

The truth is, I can hardly wait for my husband and me to have bodies made in heaven! My husband has heart problems, suffers from diabetes, and now is blind. I am deaf, I am overweight, I have a balance center disorder and three different sleep disorders, and I've suffered severe depression. But one day I will have a new body with a label on the back of my neck that says, "Made in Heaven." I'm looking forward to that day! Until then, I want to take care of my body while resting in the truth that God has saved my soul.

Except for Jesus Christ alone, God has never used a perfect woman or man in His service. In fact, God will never use anyone except those who are imperfect and flawed.

God's beloved include those who feel flawed, frail, handicapped; who are hurting and wounded; who have emotional and mental illnesses; who have personality quirks and physical imperfections. But, far more importantly, these men and women have a heart for God and great worth in His eyes—and they are spiritually beautiful.

The truth is, *you* are one of God's beloved. As you receive His love and understand the worth you have in Him, you will radiate His beauty. You will be a woman after His own heart.

◦ Prayer ◦

Lord, I am so grateful that You don't judge by appearance or height . . . For You don't see things the way we see them. Even if people judge me by my outward appearance, Lord, You look at my heart. Has fussing in front of the mirror ever made me taller by so much as an inch? All this time and money wasted on fashion—do I think it makes that much difference? Instead of looking at the fashions, I'll walk out into the fields and look at the wildflowers. They never primp or shop, and I have never seen color and design quite like it. O God, since you give such attention to the appearance of wildflowers—most of which are never seen—shouldn't I think You'll attend to me, take pride in me, do Your best for me? What You are trying to do here is to get me to relax, to not be so preoccupied with getting, so I can respond to Your giving. People who don't know You and the way You work fuss over these things, but I know You, God, and I know how You work. So help me to steep my life in God-reality, God-initiative, God-provisions. Then I won't worry about missing out on the things I need.

—BASED ON 1 SAMUEL 16:7 NLT, MATTHEW 6:25-33 MSG

↜ *Practicing the Spiritual Life* ↝

1. What, if anything, makes you feel so bad about yourself that you sometimes have trouble receiving God's love for you? What is the source of those feelings—God or other people—and why is that source important to recognize?

2. What statements of God's truth in this chapter help you see yourself at least a little bit more clearly with God's eyes?

3. If feelings of shame or inferiority ever keep you from believing that God has plans for you to serve Him, which of His promises will you embrace so you can see God's plans for you in a new way?

4. Will you say: *No matter how inferior and unworthy I feel, no matter how difficult my life, no matter what others think about me or my appearance, I will believe that God loves me and is transforming me into a woman with a heart for Him?* What are your feelings about making this commitment? What encouragement do you find in the prayer "I believe; help my unbelief" (Mark 9:24 ESV)?

Part Two

THE

CHANGED

LIFE

CHAPTER 3

FIND REST FOR YOUR SOUL

Come to me, all you who are weary
and burdened, and I will give you rest.
Take my yoke upon you and learn from me,
for I am gentle and humble in heart,
and you will find rest for your souls.
For my yoke is easy, and my burden is light.

—Matthew 11:28-30

Another overpacked day. I realize I'm running late. Again. So I grab a liquid breakfast, glance at my ransacked living room, and tell my husband I'm leaving for a doctor's appointment. But my husband has dropped the remote control for the lights. Since he is legally blind, he needs me to find it. I dig it out from under the chair and hand it to him. He reminds me we are out of milk.

After an hour in the waiting room, I finally get in to see my doctor. Then I hurry to get groceries before I pick up my granddaughters from school. I avoid the longest line at the store, but the person in front of me takes a long time to check out.

I am a couple of minutes late picking up the girls. I have a writing deadline to meet, but when we get home, the girls are especially needy and hungry. They interrupt me so often I finally give up on trying to concentrate. Then it's an evening of homework, dinner, and attempts to help my oldest granddaughter with spelling.

When I get into bed at night, the dishes aren't done and the house is a cluttered mess. I have little hope for true *rest* and many thoughts about the few hours of sleep I'll be able to squeeze in before it all begins again.

Does any of this sound familiar to you? Do you, like me, hunger for rest—not just physical rest, but for a peacefulness in the midst of chaos, a trust in the midst of uncertainty?

That's exactly what God wants for you too.

The truth is, drawing closer to the Lover of our soul always begins with resting in Him. God longs for our commitment to Him to flow from our love relationship with Him. He wants us to lean against Him, to know Him better, to be as comfortable with Him as two lovers are with each other.

Let's begin by getting to know this God who offers us, no matter our circumstances, rest for our souls.

"ALL . . . WHO ARE WEARY AND BURDENED"

Just as we do, Jesus Himself hungered for rest and spiritual refuge.

Once when He was weary after ministering to the crowds, Jesus offered this invitation to His disciples: "'Come with me by yourselves to a quiet place and get some rest.' So they went away by themselves in a boat to a solitary place" (Mark 6:31–32).

In the same way Jesus calls us: "Come to me, all you who are weary and burdened, and I will give you rest. Take my yoke upon you and learn from me, for I am gentle and humble in heart, and you will find rest for your souls. For my yoke is easy and my burden is light" (Matthew 11:28-30).

Long ago I learned those verses, but I didn't hear them as Jesus's personal invitation to me, an invitation to find rest for my soul, to hear God with my heart, and to listen to His Word until I found spiritual rest. And I often questioned how Jesus's yoke could be easy to carry and His burden light when so much suffering and evil darken our world.

But the rest God offers is not an earthly rest free from difficult circumstances and relationships. God's rest is beyond circumstances. The rest God offers is a deep peace in our soul.

God's rest is also a freedom from the guilt and shame of sin. Sin's heavy yoke overburdens us, but Christ's light yoke redeems us with forgiveness and grace. God assures us, "It is for freedom that Christ has set us free. Stand firm, then, and do not let yourselves be burdened again by a yoke of slavery" (Galatians 5:1).

In Isaiah we read, "In repentance and rest is your salvation, in quietness and trust is your strength" (Isaiah 30:15). True repentance and true rest always go together.

Resting in Christ also enables me to face trials because it helps me let go of my need for answers and frees me to trust in God's sovereignty. Resting in Christ helps me recognize that God is in control even when I feel completely out of control. I am reminded once again that it is God's power, not mine, that will bring change to my life.

"I WILL GIVE YOU REST"

Why does Christ ask us to come to Him when we're discouraged and burdened rather than just when we're rested and spiritually renewed? Jesus invites us to come when we're low because He desires to encourage us and strengthen our faith. He longs to give us relief from our physical, mental, and emotional pain. He wants us to have respite from the unrelenting heartaches that exhaust us.

Our Lord knows that we'll never feel fully at rest during our earthly journey. He also knows that most of what we do daily to maintain our lives and even much of what we do for pleasure leaves us tired. God knows that to escape our pain and those empty, lonely moments, we overload our days with meaningless activities and anxious thoughts that wear us out.

Knowing us so intimately, Christ calls us to come to Him when we're tired so He can give us rest from difficult human relationships and responsibilities, so He can relieve us of the burdens we bear, so He can refresh us when we're weary of the daily work we must do. We read in Hebrews: "For anyone who enters God's rest also rests from his own work, just as God did from his. Let us, therefore, make every effort to enter that rest" (Hebrews 4:10–11).

But how do we receive the rest God has for us? How do we draw closer to the Lover of our soul? Christ's first instruction to us is to *come*. He is calling us, and we simply need to follow. As Charles Spurgeon said, "Observe it is nothing but that one word, 'Come.' It is not 'Do'; it is not even 'Learn.' It is not 'Take up my yoke'; that will follow after, but must never be forced out of its proper place. To obtain the first rest, the rest which is a matter of gift—all that is asked of you is that you come to have it."[9]

In other seasons of my life, I had the opportunity to go on quiet retreats. Whenever I went away for a day or two, it always took me some time to get prepared to listen and respond to the Holy Spirit speaking to me through the Word of God. Though the setting would be tranquil, I started my time battling turbulent thoughts and frantic feelings that refused to settle. It would take me a couple hours or more before my spirit started to quiet and I could concentrate on the Bible or other readings.

To calm my spirit, I would sit quietly outdoors, walk in nature, pray, confess my sins, and read Scripture and spiritual classics. Still, I constantly struggled to silence my mind and to listen for what God was saying to me as I was reading. I often took naps to get the mental and physical rest I needed. After that, I was more alert and better able to hear the Lord through His Word.

During my retreat, God would convict me of the things I was doing wrong and the idols in my life. That is when I wrestled in prayer and pleaded with God to deliver me from the things that tempted me. Helpless to change on my own, to repent and be freed, I cried out to Him to transform me. God also used those weekend retreats to strengthen me to face the difficulties of my normal everyday life. He enabled me to rely on Him with renewed confidence in the truth that He was working in me and would carry me through day by day.

Of course, having such an extended time away is rare for most of us. But even during our "ordinary" times with God, at the beginning or the end of a full day, our loving Shepherd desires to lead us to green meadows beside still waters so He can cleanse our thoughts, heal our damaged lives, and restore our souls. He longs to guide us through the valley of pain, to free us from our fear of evil, to comfort us with His rod and staff. He yearns to lead us along the path of righteousness for His name's sake (Psalm 23).

Time with God does not need to be a work you labor to achieve. Instead, time with God is time for letting go, for, specifically, letting go of what you want from God and opening yourself to what He wants to do in you. It is Him working in you, not you working hard to find rest, that brings spiritual renewal.

The Lord Himself invites you to follow Him to a place of peaceful quietness for your personal restoration, to a place of solitude for your spiritual recuperation. Come! Sit at the place He has set for you. He longs to care for you, so let His healing Word ease your aching heart. Let His tender care refresh your starved soul and quench your thirst for hope and peace. Let His gracious love renew your spirit.

Come.

∽ *Prayer* ∿

Lord, in my heart I plan my own course, but You determine my steps . . . I know, O Lord, that my life is not my own; it is not for me to direct my steps . . . Teach me to do Your will, for You are my God; may Your good Spirit lead me on level ground . . . Then I will know that I can set my heart at rest in Your presence.

—PROVERBS 16:9; JEREMIAH 10:23; PSALM 143:10; 1 JOHN 3:19

∽ *Practicing the Spiritual Life* ∿

1. What do you long to experience in your relationship with the Lord?

2. What kind of rest does Jesus offer you?

3. In what areas of your life do you need personal and spiritual rest? Picture God surveying each of those areas and saying to you, "Come to Me." How would you feel if He said, "I'll fix all those areas for you" instead of simply saying, "Come"?

4. What does God's desire for you to come to Him reveal about His desires for you?

CHAPTER 4

RECEIVE GOD'S GRACE

For it is by grace you have been saved,
through faith—and this not from yourselves,
it is the gift of God—not by works,
so that no one can boast.

—*Ephesians 2:8-9*

The flooded Amagu River was deeper, stronger, and more treacherous than Bob Conrad had anticipated. A missionary in Papua New Guinea, he had just completed a twelve-village visit in the East Sepik Province. Now he waited to cross the river, hoping the water would go down so he could return home.

After waiting more than an hour, he drove his motorbike to a place where he'd crossed the river many times before. He rode down the bank into the water, but the engine sputtered and died. Suddenly the swift current swept Bob downstream.

Still on his bike, he desperately tried to reach shore. Then he fell, and the bike pinned him underwater. He fought to reach the surface, but the raging river and the weight of his bike, backpack, helmet, and a heavily loaded bag kept pulling him under.

Quickly losing strength, he prayed, "Lord, help me!"

A young man passing by saw Bob's plight and rushed down the riverbank. Benny Gabriel tried to pull the struggling man out of the water, but he couldn't do it alone. Then a surge of water from upstream swelled the tumultuous river, making it even more dangerous.

Three of Benny's friends arrived at the scene and rushed to help him. The men formed a human chain, linked hands, and pulled Bob ashore. Later, the local people told Bob that it was the first time anyone caught in the floodwaters of the Amagu River had survived.[10]

SAVING GRACE

In this story we see a picture of God's saving grace. Without faith in Christ, we are caught in the world's floodwaters and dragged under by the heavy backpack of sin. Though we may struggle to reach safety by ourselves, the weight of sin—the ways we keep missing the mark—will continue to pull us under. We do not have the strength to save ourselves. All our efforts are futile, but when we cry out to the Lord to rescue us, He reaches down and carries us safely to shore.

The truth, spiritually speaking, is that we cannot save ourselves. Some people think they have to work their way into heaven by earning God's favor. They have to wait until they are a "better" person or change their behavior in order for God to accept them.

How are we saved? How can we have a personal relationship with God? By believing that Jesus is our Savior, and through Him we receive forgiveness for our wrongdoing and eternal life with Him.

Believing in Jesus is so simple that many people question it. You can come to God just as you are right now. You don't have to work for your faith. You don't have to read the entire Bible or change who you are as a person. You don't have to feel a certain way. If you are skeptical, ask God to make Himself clear to you and to give you faith enough to believe. He will!

Here is a prayer using Scripture that you can offer to God to express your belief in Christ:

O God, You are faithful and reliable. I confess my sins; please forgive them and cleanse me from everything I've done wrong. Jesus, I confess with my mouth that You are Lord and believe in my heart that God raised You from the dead, so that I can be saved. For it is by believing in my heart that I am made right with You, God, and it is by confessing with my mouth that I am saved. (1 John 1:9 GW; Romans 10:9–10 NLT)

If you have prayed this prayer, welcome to your new life in Jesus Christ. Now look to Him to guide you as you learn more about God and how He works in our lives.

A CALL TO HOLINESS

God calls us to be holy, but what exactly does that mean? *Holiness* is a heavenly word that is difficult to comprehend. Trying to define it in earthly terms is similar to trying to translate a word from one language into another. How, for example, would we translate the word *computer* into the native language of a people who have never seen a computer and have no electrical equipment? A picture of a computer would be as meaningless to them as any words we might use.

Similarly, how do we translate the heavenly word *holiness* so it makes sense in our world? We begin to understand holiness as we draw closer to the Lover of our soul, and the way we do that is to realize that we who follow Christ do not belong to this world (John 15:19). We're "aliens and strangers" whose language, culture, and lifestyle should be different from people who do belong. We're God's people and citizens of heaven (1 Peter 2:10-11; Philippians 3:20).

Yet how often we reflect God's holy ways one moment, but in the next moment realize our actions or thoughts are horrifyingly sinful! How many of us confess a sin, vow never to do it again, and then all too quickly commit that same sin? Our failure rate—the rate at which we sin—may be so high that we wonder if we'll ever become a woman with a heart for God. In fact, leading a holy life may seem so difficult that we give up even trying.

But before you give up, consider a few saints:

Moses murdered an Egyptian, fled to the desert, and spent forty years in exile herding sheep. Moses "was afraid to look at God" when He spoke to Moses from the burning bush. He was so terrified he asked God to choose someone else to lead the Israelites (Exodus 3:6; 4:13).

David committed adultery with Bathsheba and then devised a plan to have her husband murdered (2 Samuel 11-12). Later, seventy thousand men of Israel died in a plague because David conducted an unauthorized census of his troops (2 Samuel 24).

The woman at the well was a prostitute who'd had five husbands, and she was not married to the man she was living with (John 4:1-18).

Three times Peter betrayed Jesus by denying that he knew Him (Matthew 26:69-75).

Saul of Tarsus persecuted Christians and consented to the stoning of Stephen. He later confessed, "For I am the least of the apostles and do not even deserve to be called an apostle, because I persecuted the church of God. But by the grace of God I am what I am, and his grace to me was not without effect. No, I worked harder than all of them—yet not I, but the grace of God that was with me" (1 Corinthians 15:9-10).

Those flawed characters had sinned in biblical proportions, but God still accomplished His will through their lives. Why was that possible? Because they recognized their need for God's grace.

Charles Swindoll wrote this about Paul (formerly Saul): "By realizing that he did not deserve and could never earn the privileges given him, Paul was freed to be exactly who he was and do precisely what he was called to do. Grace became his silent partner, his constant traveling companion, his invisible security, since he (in himself) was in no way deserving of the part he played in God's unfolding drama."[11]

We are equally undeserving. But God's call to holiness can free us rather than paralyze us. May our awareness of sin not defeat us but drive us to repent and reconcile ourselves to Christ so we may be free to live by His grace.

Our hope is in this promise: "Where sin increased, grace increased all the more, so that, just as sin reigned in death, so also grace might reign through righteousness to bring eternal life through Jesus Christ our Lord" (Romans 5:20-21). But does the fact that an increase of sin prompts an increase in grace mean "we go on sinning so that grace may increase? By no means!" (Romans 6:1-2).

Instead of letting sin in our life increase, we are to rely on the Holy Spirit to strengthen us through the transforming power of God's amazing grace. We must also remember that we are called to live holy, sanctified lives—continually dying to our sins, rising to newness of life, and being changed further into Christ's image—and we cannot do so without the grace of God working in us.

CHEAP GRACE VS. COSTLY GRACE

This truth is so important that I want to say it again: God's grace saves us. Faith in Christ is a gift, and all we need to do is accept it with gratitude. It's not a reward. We cannot earn it, work for it, or brag about it (Ephesians 2:8–9). That truth is foundational to our Christian faith. We may feel driven to work hard for God, to be involved in everything at church, or to devote ourselves to ministry to win favor with God. On the other hand, we may think that we're safe to do as we please because we'll get to heaven anyway.

Here we confront the stark differences between "cheap grace" and "costly grace." As German pastor Dietrich Bonhoeffer put it, "Cheap grace is the grace we bestow on ourselves. . . . Cheap grace is grace without discipleship, grace without the cross, grace without Jesus Christ, living and incarnate."[12]

We're living by cheap grace when we do whatever we please without any sense of responsibility to the Lord. If we remain in an apathetic spiritual condition and refuse to deal with our sins, we'll become hardened and insensitive to our need for constant spiritual renewal.

If we keep resisting the Holy Spirit's conviction to change, we won't submit ourselves to the lifelong process of transformation. We won't be committed to a disciplined spiritual life, personal discipleship, and service. Christ may be our Savior, but He is not our Lord and Master. That's cheap grace!

By contrast, Bonhoeffer continued, "Grace is costly because it calls us to follow Jesus Christ. It is costly because it costs a man his life, and it is grace because it gives a man the only true life. It is costly because it condemns sin, and grace because it justifies the sinner. . . . Costly grace confronts us as a gracious call to follow Jesus; it comes as a word of forgiveness to the broken spirit and the contrite heart."[13]

I struggle with many frailties and failures. I continually battle depression, worry, overeating, and overworking. But the costly grace of following Jesus means that I allow God's strength to show even in my weaknesses: "My grace is sufficient for you, for my power is made perfect in weakness" (2 Corinthians 12:9).

Costly grace calls us to be transformed by the Holy Spirit's power and the Word of God throughout our entire lifetime. Costly grace holds us accountable to repent and change, to be more Christlike, more faithful, and more fruitful.

Costly grace pushes us out of our comfortable places and challenges us to be open each day to opportunities to minister to others. Costly grace means giving and living sacrificially . . . for the good of God's people and for His glory.

HEAVENLY GRACE

The Bible and many Christian books, especially the spiritual classics, set high standards for godliness, but few of us consistently reach those goals. I fail miserably despite my desire to live the disciplined spiritual life. I sin daily even though I don't want to, and I do so either deliberately or without meaning to.

Even the apostle Paul knew this struggle: "We know that the law is spiritual; but I am unspiritual, sold as a slave to sin. I do not understand what I do. For what I want to do I do not do, but what I hate I do.... I know that nothing good lives in me, that is, in my sinful nature. For I have the desire to do what is good, but I cannot carry it out" (Romans 7:14-15, 18).

God desires us to let go of our failures and sins, past and present. He continues to pursue us no matter how many times we fall. He sees our sin more clearly than we do. He thoroughly understands that we are broken people—and He desires to glorify Himself in us and through us despite our brokenness.

As paradoxical as it may seem, God is more honored by humble servants, broken by their own sin as well as by hard times in this fallen world, than by believers who consider themselves spiritually competent, if not spiritually superior.

The Lord has promised us the power of His grace and His Holy Spirit to enable us to live in accordance with what He desires. We may repeatedly fail to meet our spiritual goals and, more importantly, His holy standards for us, but we can keep pressing on, keep on surrendering to His disciplining and training hand. If we surrender to God, He will strengthen our commitment to Him, empower us to serve, and thereby build our faith.

Consider this analogy: I have an extremely painful physical condition that has plagued me off and on for fifty-five years. The doctor has told me, "It's treatable but not curable." Despite the constant medical treatments I undergo and the highly restricted regimen I follow, the pain persists, limiting my activities and exhausting me. At its worst, the pain is barely manageable.

In a similar way, while we're here on earth, spiritual weaknesses may be treatable but not curable. The pain we experience as a result of a fallen fleshly nature is excruciating and exhausting. The hurt may seem unmanageable, and our effectiveness for God limited. Faithful obedience and submission to God is the only sure treatment, and it has to be administered minute by waking minute.

I appreciate Charles Swindoll's candid remarks on this subject: "Another undeniable struggle all of us live with is our own human weaknesses, which crop up any number of ways again and again. We suffer. We hurt. We fail. We blow it. We feel bad. Medication won't relieve it. Prayer doesn't remove it. Complaining doesn't help it. Our problem? We are just human! Imperfection dogs our steps."[14]

That fact explains why every one of us fights a daily battle against sin. And that's where God steps in. Receiving His grace means trusting that He is sufficient when we are deficient.

And although we are imperfect, we fail, and we are weak, we may—by God's grace—look forward to a whole new life one day. Paul knew pain on this earth, but he proclaimed: "Our citizenship is in heaven. And we eagerly await a Savior from there, the Lord Jesus Christ, who, by the power that enables him to bring everything under his control, will transform our lowly bodies so that they will be like his glorious body" (Philippians 3:20-21). We will no longer be plagued by the addictions, ailments, sins, and weaknesses that currently weigh us down. There *is* a cure!

And here's a great promise to hold on to while we await that day: "'Behold, I will create new heavens and a new earth. The former things will not be remembered, nor will they come to mind'" (Isaiah 65:17).

When we reach heaven, "there will be no more death or mourning or crying or pain" (Revelation 21:4), and we'll experience the wondrous freedom of being holy forevermore. We'll live with our glorious Savior in a magnificent heavenly universe: we cannot begin to imagine the wonders awaiting us. Now that's grace!

∾ *Prayer* ∾

Jesus, because I believe in You, I am freed from all guilt and declared right with God—something the Jewish law could not do for me . . . So sin shall not be my master, because I am not under law, but under grace. What then? Shall I sin because I am not under law but under grace? By no means! . . . I will not set aside Your grace, for if righteousness could be gained through the law, Jesus, You died for nothing! . . . You were handed over to die because of my sins, and You were raised from the dead to make me right with God . . . And, Almighty God, having been made right in Your sight, I have peace with You because of what Jesus has done for me. Because of my faith, Jesus has brought me into this place of highest privilege where I now stand, and I confidently and joyfully look forward to sharing in His glory . . . Until that day, may Your grace continue to be poured out on me abundantly, filling me with faith and love for Christ Jesus.

—ACTS 13:39 NLT; ROMANS 6:14-15; GALATIANS 2:21;
ROMANS 4:25; 5:1-2 NLT; 1 TIMOTHY 1:14

∾ *Practicing the Spiritual Life* ∾

1. How can we have a personal relationship with God? What do you believe about Jesus Christ?

2. What are the differences between cheap grace and costly grace? What does God's grace personally mean to you?

3. Why can God's grace actually motivate you to obey Him?

4. What do you most appreciate about God's gift of grace?

CHAPTER 5

RESPOND TO GOD'S LOVE

Love the LORD your God with all your heart
and with all your soul and with all your strength.
—Deuteronomy 6:5

Maybe you're like me: you know the reasons for maintaining intentional time with God, but you find it hard to do day in and day out. Still, the Lord, as the Lover of our soul, continues to draw us to Himself.

He invites us to come feast with Him at His banquet table: "Listen, listen to me, and eat what is good, and your soul will delight in the richest of fare. Give ear and come to me; hear me, that your soul may live" (Isaiah 55:2-3).

Just as we take time to prepare food for our physical health and well-being, we need to take time to nourish our spiritual life. Spending quiet time alone with God is truly essential to our spiritual well-being. It increases my faith, reduces my worry, and makes me more aware of what God desires to do in my life.

PERSONAL TIME WITH THE LORD

Most believers know it's important to have a "devotional life," but sometimes just the word *devotions* can make us feel guilty. We think of how inconsistent we are or how we rush through our time with the

Lord. We worry that we're spiritual failures because we don't do our devotions a certain way.

Then there are those times when we sit down to pray and read our Bible, but we're so tired we can barely focus on the words, let alone concentrate on their meaning. If our mind wanders and we can't concentrate, if we don't seem to get anything out of what we're reading, or if we don't feel any different afterward, we wonder, *Why bother?*

I used to think I'd failed when I came away from my quiet time still feeling spiritually empty. I now realize that my feelings have little to do with what God is doing in my life. I now want to spend time with God to build our relationship just as I want to spend time with my husband, sons, and grandchildren to build our relationship—and simply because I love them and enjoy being with them.

But I don't always feel that way about having devotions. It's easy to let routine obligations hinder us when we feel less than excited about spending time with the Lord. I certainly do! That's why the habit of reading my Bible and praying often begins by asking the Lord for the desire.

I have also come to realize that we cannot develop or maintain a spiritual life by ourselves. During most of my Christian life, I have prayed with one or two people on a regular basis. We need encouragers like that who help us keep up the pace, whose example and support inspire us to continue our walk with the Lord even when we don't feel we can put one foot in front of the other. It gives us strength to "know that we are not alone or forgotten as we run the race, especially when the stretch of road we are on grows long and lonely."[15]

When the road does get long or hard, it helps to remind ourselves why we develop a spiritual life. Here are a few reasons that I've discovered:

First, our spiritual life starts with God. He is the Initiator, and He draws us to Himself. God's love is the richest incentive and greatest motive for us to consistently spend time with Him.

The good news is that God's love comes to us by His choice, not ours:

- "This is love: not that we loved God, but that he loved us and sent his Son as an atoning sacrifice for our sins" (1 John 4:10).
- "God lives in us and his love is made complete in us" (1 John 4:12).
- "We love because he first loved us" (1 John 4:19).

Our love for God comes as a response to God's love for us:

- "Be imitators of God, therefore, as dearly loved children and live a life of love, just as Christ loved us and gave himself up for us as a fragrant offering and sacrifice to God" (Ephesians 5:1-2).
- "Love the LORD your God with all your heart and with all your soul and with all your strength" (Deuteronomy 6:5 and echoed in Deuteronomy 10:12 and Matthew 22:37).

Second, a devotional life helps us to obey a command that is stated ten different times throughout the Bible: "love your neighbor as yourself" (Leviticus 19:18). In addition to calling us to love our neighbor, who may or may not believe in God, the Lord also commands us to love those who *do* know Him.

In fact, the entire book of 1 John is a love commandment to Christians: "Love one another . . . If we love one another, God lives in us and his love is made complete in us" (1 John 4:11-12).

A rich devotional life enables us to love not just brothers and sisters in Christ but strangers as well. In the Old Testament, God told the Israelites to treat an alien as they would their own: "Love him as yourself, for you were aliens in Egypt" (Leviticus 19:34). In the New Testament as well, the Lord directs us to show kindness to strangers (Matthew 25:35).

Jesus calls us to "love your enemies and pray for those who persecute you" (Matthew 5:44). Hatred, prejudice, and judgmental attitudes are not to characterize God's people. Instead, we are to offer acceptance, compassion, and love, and when we do so, we are giving to others the same grace, kindness, and mercy Jesus gives us.

Yes, God commands us to love the Father, Son, and Holy Spirit. He commands us to love Christians and non-Christians, family members and friends, neighbors and strangers, allies and opponents: "Love each other deeply, because love covers over a multitude of sins" (1 Peter 4:8).

Love, however, doesn't come naturally. So our quiet times are an opportunity for the Lord to grow and strengthen in our heart and mind a love for others that will then, by His grace, be reflected in our words and actions.

When we meet with our Lord, we can confess how we struggle to love those who we don't like, who are difficult, or who behave in destructive ways. We can freely ask the Lord to show us how to love neighbors we may not even know; how to love people when we disagree with their choices; how to love those who wound us deeply; and how to love prodigals who have distanced themselves from us as well as from their heavenly Father.

Like the father of the prodigal, for instance, we need to release our loved ones who have gone their own way and pour out our concerns for them through prayer as we watch and wait for them to come home to their Father.

Although Christ calls us to love others, we need to realize that He alone can give us compassionate love for the unlovable people in our lives. During our times with Him, He is able to heal our pain and enable us to love when we don't have any love to give.

Third, we need to develop spiritually so we can "serve one another in love" (Galatians 5:13). We also should use whatever gift we have "received to serve others, faithfully administering God's grace in its various forms" (1 Peter 4:10).

Love is sacrificial, but caring for our family and others should not make them feel as if they are in debt to us. Instead, by God's grace and as a result of His transforming work in our lives, those we serve will receive our acts of love with joy.

Finally, spending time with God offers us the opportunity to confess our sins so that we might have a clean heart and a right spirit before our Lord. Admission, confession, and repentance are three steps involved in overcoming sin.

THE ULTIMATE GOAL

It's absolutely true that we cannot lead godly lives in our own power. God is the One who helps us embrace the beauty of a life devoted to Him. As we faithfully meet with Jesus, He enables us to face trials of all kinds, He guides our steps and strengthens our faith, and He uses us to comfort others with the comfort we have received from Him.

During tough times, God teaches us how to trust Him more, provides spiritual refreshment, establishes constancy in our journey, and makes us more aware of His caring presence with us.

Furthermore, regular time with the Lord is key to our staying in communication with Him, whether through prayer, worship, or praise. God longs for us to listen to His Spirit, to seek and experience His guidance, and to ask for spiritual wisdom, understanding, and insights about our daily life. God wants us to be in this kind of intimate relationship with Him.

～ *Prayer* ～

Kind and loving LORD, satisfy me in the morning with Your unfailing love, that I may sing for joy and be glad . . . Remember, O LORD, your great mercy and love, for they are from of old." . . . "I will remember the deeds of the LORD; yes, I will remember your miracles of long ago. I will meditate on all your works and consider all your mighty deeds." . . . I acknowledge You, God, and will serve You with wholehearted devotion and with a willing mind, for You search my heart and understand every motive behind my thoughts . . . Father God, I will come and listen to You; for You will teach me to revere and worshipfully fear You . . . I will receive the law from Your mouth and lay up Your words in my heart. For then I will delight in You, Almighty One, and will lift up my face to You, O God.

—PSALM 90:14; 25:6; 77:11-12; 1 CHRONICLES 28:9; PSALM 34:11 AMP; JOB 22:22, 26

✎ *Practicing the Spiritual Life* ✎

1. Describe your spiritual life right now. In what ways would you like it to change or not change?

2. Ask the Lord to show you specific ways to express love to one person you find difficult to care about. Make a commitment to show that person God's love sometime this week.

3. Ask the Lord to reveal areas of sin in your life, remembering that He desires to deliver you and transform you.

4. What was one Scripture verse in this chapter that stood out to you? Talk to God about why that verse resonates with you. Then listen for how He wants to use this truth in your life.

5. We meet with the Lord so He can change us into His image. In order to conform to His image, what habits of thinking do you need to change? Be specific and then ask for His help.

CHAPTER 6

SPEND TIME WITH GOD

The plans of the LORD stand firm forever,
the purposes of his heart through all generations.

—*Psalm 33:11*

When I was a girl, I loved watching butterflies. They dance in the air as gracefully as ballerinas. They glide and pirouette and soar to their own melodies. Their beauty is enchanting.

But then I captured one.

When I brushed the iridescent wings, the glorious orange-and-black colors turned to dust. Soon the wings could no longer fly.

I realized that butterflies are fragile and delicate: they quickly die when they're mishandled.

Developing a spiritual life reminds me of trying to catch an elusive butterfly. We may capture godliness for a moment, but then it seems to die in our hands. No matter how much we may desire to lead God-honoring lives, we can never capture those qualities without their glorious colors turning to dusty gray. Even the slightest brush with sin tarnishes the beauty of holiness. Ungodly thoughts. A self-protective lie. A few unkind words. A rude, inconsiderate reaction. A refusal to help someone in need.

It's these inconsistencies in our lives that seem to defeat us. We do wrong things daily, hourly, and moment by moment. How can we ever become a woman with a heart for God?

DEVELOPING YOUR SPIRITUAL LIFE

Personal transformation comes through a gradual but consistent commitment to exercise our faith and open our hearts to God's desires and His Word. We realize that we cannot change ourselves. Instead, we must surrender ourselves to the Lord and be open to His work in our hearts and in our lives.

A friend shared with me that she works long hours and feels guilty because she just doesn't have time to sit down and have devotions. As I shared about the various ways we can spend time with the Lord, she mentioned that every morning she listens to a favorite pastor on the radio as she gets ready for work and prays as she drives to the office. As we were talking, she realized that she *was* being intentional in her relationship with God.

There are many ways to spend time with God, and it's important to follow a plan that considers our current commitments, our interests, and life's pressing needs. But we must be wary of developing a consistent time with God that only satisfies our personal desires instead of following the Lord's directions.

How often do we come to our quiet time with our hearts and minds focused on everything else but the Lord, as He describes in this verse: "These people come near to me with their mouth and honor me with their lips, but their hearts are far from me" (Isaiah 29:13).

Sometimes I come before the Lord intending just to read a quick devotional and then do what I want to do. So I only halfway pay attention to the words as I read, or I stop in the middle and never finish. My heart is far from God, and I'm much too focused on my own needs. After several days like this, of course my relationship with Him becomes shallow.

It's key for us to be teachable and willing to lift our eyes off ourselves and then turn to our Lord who transforms us. Many times the Lord prompts me to read a certain Bible passage or devotion or book so that He can either speak to me in a specific way or give me the guidance or assurance I need.

I've also found that my simply having a planned time to be with God gives the Holy Spirit freedom to work. When I keep showing up, I also become more attuned to God's voice speaking to me through whatever I read that day. When we listen for His voice, we can be amazed by how He guides us.

As we read in the previous chapter, a key reason for maintaining a consistent time with the Lord is to enable us to know and love God so intimately that we can serve others in a godly, loving way. When we intentionally and regularly draw closer to God, we grow in our desire to obey Him, and we more easily recognize His presence with us in all we do.

PLANNING OUR TIME WITH GOD

Spending time with the Lord to study His Word grows our faith and teaches us how to surrender to His will for our lives. "All Scripture is inspired by God and is useful to teach us what is true and to make us realize what is wrong in our lives. It corrects us when we are wrong and teaches us to do what is right" (2 Timothy 3:16 NLT).

Using His Word, God guides us, gives us wisdom, and teaches us His ways and His will. God is constantly reaching out to us, speaking to us through His Word and His Spirit. We need to open our heart, listen, and respond.

Here are some options to consider as you develop a devotional plan:

- Do a Bible study.
- Read through the Bible in a year.
- Use a daily devotional booklet.
- Read a nonfiction Christian book written in an inspirational style (Philip Keller's *A Shepherd Looks at Psalm 23*) or in an instructive style (Jerry Bridges' *The Pursuit of Holiness*). Look for titles from Max Lucado, Philip Yancey, C. S. Lewis, and Tim Keller as well.
- Study the Bible along with a variety of other books, commentaries, or devotionals.
- Learn all that the Bible says about a certain topic.
- Dig deep into the meaning of a single passage.
- Study a chapter from the Bible.
- Tackle a detailed chapter-by-chapter or verse-by-verse analysis of a specific book of the Bible.

Now let's sharpen the focus on a few of the items in the above list. If, for instance, you want to do a Bible study, do you want one that lasts six weeks, eight weeks, or longer? Do you like studies written in an easy narrative style or those that wrestle with deep theological issues? Do you prefer studies that you just read or ones that require you to write out answers?

You may enjoy the spiritual classics or a devotional with a single-page daily story that teaches a lesson you can apply to your life. Maybe you don't enjoy reading at all. Instead, you prefer to listen to Christian music, sermons from a pastor you enjoy, radio broadcasts from a favorite teacher, or Bible studies from a local church downloaded on your iPod.

Having thought about the *what*, now consider the *where*. Finding a place that is not cluttered with things that demand your attention is a good first step toward making time to be with God. Set aside a corner if that is all you have and let it be a sanctuary where you meet with the Lord. If you have your devotions when you first wake up, have something light to eat so you don't constantly think about being hungry.

If you can find a safe setting, having devotions outdoors is a wonderful way to get in touch with our Creator Lord. (A friend of mine leaves for work early, sits in her car next to a park, and spends time with God.) Whichever option you choose, be sure to turn off your phone so you have a few minutes without interruption.

Even after considering the above possibilities, you may not be sure what you prefer or which would work best in your life right now. Moreover, what God determines we need today might be different from what we'll need tomorrow. So I encourage you to try different ways to meet with God until you discover the ones that excite you and make you want to spend more time with your Savior and Lord. Be creative—and, again, be listening for His direction.

DISCOVERING THE MANY WAYS
TO SPEND TIME WITH THE LORD

You've already read about a number of the many different ways to spend time with the Lord, to strengthen your walk with God. And here are more:

- Keep in touch with God throughout the day by praying when you're driving to and from work, going to appointments, or running errands. Pray silently or aloud. Practice listening to the Lord. He is speaking to us all the time, initiating prayer times, nudging us to intercede for others, and prompting us to be aware of those many divine appointments He sets before us.

- Write a scripture verse or passage on several index cards and place them on your nightstand, in your bathroom, or above the kitchen sink. When you notice the cards as you go about your day, reflect on the meaning of the verses or practice memorizing them. Change the cards regularly.

- Listen to Christian radio programs or put Christian music or messages on your iPod.

- Grow along with your children by reading a children's Bible with them. In the car, sing choruses with your children, listen to story or music CDs with them, or play simple Bible games. (With young children, for instance, play "Guess Who?": "Who used a slingshot to kill a giant? What was the giant's name?") You'll be surprised at how you can use simple Bible stories to show how God is working in your family today.

- Learn to pay attention to what is going on and listen for the Lord to speak to you in the circumstances of your life. He speaks to us in many ways—often about the same thing!

    Perhaps you first hear an idea in a conversation, then you hear the same point made in a sermon, after which a friend "randomly" texts you a verse that corresponds to that idea, and then you overhear someone saying the same thing at the grocery store.

    In my life, for instance, when I heard, "Be still, and know that I am God" (Psalm 46:10) from so many different places, I knew I needed to pay attention.

    Don't miss how God is working in your life—and then tell your family and others about what He's doing, and they'll be encouraged to pay attention too.

- When you know of a special concern or critical need on a particular day, such as someone having surgery, write that person's name on self-sticking notes and place them in strategic places to remind you to pray throughout the day.

- My own devotional plan also includes regularly attending church services and meeting with different Christian friends for accountability, confession, and prayer. I've also attended Bible studies and small prayer-support groups that strengthened my faith. Teaching classes—to kids or adults or ages in between—can also grow your faith.

- Have informal times of fellowship, grab a snack, eat a meal, play games, organize a church softball team, or do something fun with other Christians, and you'll find yourself spiritually refreshed. Even in relaxed settings, we can discover common needs and struggles. We also find greater hope for our own lives when we hear how God has guided others and we realize we're not alone in our troubles when others share their heartaches.

- But what about those times when we can barely muster enough strength to get out of bed in the morning? Those dark nights of the soul when we can barely pray, "Jesus, hold on to me"? Pray even if you do so woodenly. Pray even though your prayers don't seem to rise higher than the ceiling. Pray despite your anger and heartache. You'll discover what I've discovered: God *does* hold on to us. He is at our side all the time; He is present with us even when we don't realize it.

Jesus, our soon-to-be Husband, waits with us and prays for us as we deal with circumstances we can't change and pain we're not sure we can bear. Jesus is our daily Companion. He tenderly loves us. He initiates a relationship with us and waits for us to respond to Him, just like a young man who has fallen in love with the girl he wants to marry.

All of these ideas for spending time with the Lord are helpful, and when we realize that the Lover of our soul has taken the initiative to reach out to us, we find ourselves free to respond wholeheartedly to

His love. We are free to see how much He longs for an intimate relationship with us. Then the call to spend time with God is not a burden but a delight. Our spending time with Jesus is a natural response to Him who truly is the Lover of our soul.

ANGELS WATCHING OVER ME

You may think some of these suggestions are too simple. How could praying in the car or selecting verse cards from a promise box make any difference in your heart or your life?

First, realize that it's not doing one specific kind of exercise that helps us maintain spiritual fitness; it's doing many kinds of exercises.

And God uses even the simplest of spiritual practices. Many years ago during my devotions, the Lord prepared me for an unexpected trial, and then He showed me His protective presence in a very special way.

That morning I read three different passages of Scripture, in my Bible and on verse cards, that spoke of how God's angels protect us. One verse was Psalm 91:11: "He will command his angels concerning you to guard you in all your ways." After reading the passages, though, I began to feel edgy and wondered if something might happen: *Would I need the protection of God's angels today?*

At the time, I was working for a publishing company as a book editor and had a twenty-eight-mile commute. That morning at work, a promotional poster for a children's book about guardian angels arrived. The caption on the poster was "Angels Watching Over Me." I joked with another editor about reading three verses on the same topic during my devotions. But I felt concerned—until I became consumed by the busy workday and I had forgotten about the verses and the poster.

That night I left work later than usual, at about seven o'clock. When I reached my car, I saw that I had a flat tire. My husband was working out of town more than a hundred miles away. Our publishing offices were located in an isolated high-crime area, and car troubles unnerve me, so I began to feel anxious and afraid.

The security guards tried to help me, but they couldn't get the tire off because they didn't realize the hubcap was locked onto the tire. I called a friend and asked her if she could take me home, but she couldn't.

Then I called a towing service that changed the tire, but I had only a small spare. The man who changed the tire said it would be unsafe to drive twenty-eight freeway miles on the small tire, but neither he nor the security guards knew where I could get the flat tire repaired.

By now it was nearly nine fifteen. Even though the verses about God's guardian angels kept coming to my mind and even though I knew the Lord was attempting to comfort me with His words, I began to panic. I finally thought of another friend who lived nearby, and I called him to see if he knew of any place I could get the tire repaired. He came to my workplace and led me to a gas station. By then it was a quarter of ten, and the station closed at ten.

Fortunately, the mechanics at the gas station were able to repair the tire, and I made it home, exhausted but grateful that God had sent His angels of mercy to help me and watch over me. Though the flat tire turned out to be a lengthy ordeal and the Lord knows how much car trouble terrifies me, He took care of me through it all. God also reminded me of how He'd graciously prepared me during that day for such a trial—and of how He'd kept His promise to protect me.

The Lord daily shows Himself to us in numerous personal and precious ways, but we need to be looking for Him to act and listening for Him to speak. The more time we spend with God, the more clearly we realize that although our heartaches may continue and our problems may remain unchanged, our unchangeable God is near us every minute of every day to comfort us, protect us, and strengthen our faith.

ᘓ *Prayer* ᘔ

"O God, you are my God, earnestly I seek you; my soul thirsts for you, my body longs for you, in a dry and weary land where there is no water." . . . *Many are the plans of my heart, O Lord, but I know Your purpose will prevail . . . Please direct my steps, because how can I possibly understand my own way? . . . All of my ways seem right to me, but You, Lord, weigh my heart . . . I will seek Your face with all my heart, and I ask You to be gracious to me according to Your promise. I will consider my ways and turn my steps to Your statutes . . . Your thoughts are precious to me, O God! How vast is the sum of them! Were I to count Your thoughts, they would outnumber the grains of sand.*

—PSALM 63:1; PROVERBS 19:21; 20:24; 21:2; PSALM 119:58-59; 139:17-18

ᘓ *Practicing the Spiritual Life* ᘔ

1. Describe your current spiritual practices. What is your prayer life like? What is your approach to Scripture reading?

2. When has God used a simple devotional practice to draw you closer to Him? Be specific.

3. What devotional practices have most enriched your relationship with God? Why do you think those practices were helpful?

4. Comment on the value of reading about my "Angels Watching Over Me" experience and then, with humble gratitude, share details about a time you were aware of angels watching over you.

CHAPTER 7

GROW IN DIFFERENT SEASONS

I am the vine; you are the branches.
Those who remain in me, and I in them,
will produce much fruit.
For apart from me you can do nothing.

—John 15:5, NLT

Vineyards grow and flourish in the hot, dry land of Israel. So when He taught, Jesus referred to vineyards to illustrate how people grow spiritually and whether they will produce luscious fruit or bitter grapes. Interestingly, grapes often grow best in harsh weather conditions. The more the vines suffer, the better their grapes.

If you add compost to the dry, sandy soil, grapes thrive even more. Again, the harsher the conditions, the sweeter the grape. And with the right nourishment at the right time in those harsh conditions, the more fruitful the grapevine.

What a powerful metaphor for our spiritual lives! In the Song of the Vineyard in Isaiah 5:1-7, God spoke through the prophet of His great love for His people and how He chose them just as He would choose fertile land for a vineyard. In the soil of their lives, He planted His Word so they would bear an abundant harvest of fruit. He attempted to clear their minds and hearts of the stones of sin. He also built a watchtower so He could watch over and protect His people.

Then God waited and "looked for a crop of good grapes, but it yielded only bad fruit." God questioned, "What more could have been done for my vineyard than I have done for it? When I looked for good grapes, why did it yield only bad?" (Isaiah 5:2, 4).

In the biblical imagery of a vineyard, we learn about God's great care for us as well as His work in our lives so that we might bear a harvest of spiritual fruit that will glorify Him. Above all else, He longs that we flourish in our faith, and He often uses suffering to help us grow.

In John 15, Jesus told us that we're to bear fruit by remaining attached to the Vine, attached to Him. We're to follow Jesus's commands and remain in His love just as He obeys His Father's commands and remains in His Father's love.

God is the Vinedresser who tends to us as we grow into fruit-bearing branches. If we stay attached to Jesus, He nourishes us so that we may climb the sheer walls of faith and bear fruit for His glory. Even when the Lord prunes us, even when the intense heat of trials beats down on us, Jesus sustains us, tends to us, and grows us until we bear spiritual fruit for His glory and the benefit of others. If we break away from the Vine, we can do nothing. We wilt and die apart from Jesus.

REMAINING IN CHRIST

As we saw in the previous chapter, setting a time to be alone with God enables us to be more attuned to His voice. Time with Him is also a way of remaining in the Vine, and the personal and spiritual benefits are many.

I, for instance, am more at rest and at peace during the day, and I have a greater sense of the Lord's guiding presence with me when I meet with Him in the morning. I've realized, though, that where and how we spend time with the Lord changes as the seasons of life change. The demands of life and the needs of our family differ from day to day and from year to year. It takes creativity and flexibility for us to find new places, times, and ways to be with Jesus.

Snapshot I – Through the years, I've become more relaxed about having a *morning* quiet time. I make my plans with open hands, and I keep an open heart as to what God wants me to do during that time.

When I was teaching part-time in the morning, for example, I spent some quiet time with God as soon as I got up: for ten to twenty minutes, I read the Bible or another devotional book and wrote in my journal. Then, I walked in the local schoolyard for exercise. I carried index cards on which I'd written a few Scripture verses and a list of prayer requests.

I enjoyed the tranquility of my schoolyard sanctuary with the graceful elm trees lining its perimeters and the early-morning birds gathered on the grass, feeding and chirping, while the crows on the top of the telephone lines squawked their warnings that I was coming.

During those mornings, I was very flexible. Sometimes I reflected on the Scriptures and prayed the requests written on my cards, sometimes I prayed without reading the verses at all, sometimes I tried to memorize a verse or passage, and sometimes I thought through a personal concern and sought the Lord's guidance. What I did on one morning was usually different from what I had done the previous morning.

On our breakfast table, I had two calendars—one with Bible verses and another one with spiritual quotations from various Christian authors. I reflected on the calendar quotes while I was eating, and I was often amazed by how often they would either match the verses on the cards I carried in my schoolyard sanctuary or addressed a particular concern of mine. God used those calendars and cards in a variety of ways, to confirm, comfort, convict, guide, and prepare me.

My morning schedule was tight, but I felt as if I'd spent quality time with the Lord. I had read devotionally for fifteen minutes. I had prayed, sung hymns, and reflected on Scripture for twenty minutes while walking and for ten minutes during breakfast.

Snapshot II – When our sons were growing up—and now that I am helping raise our granddaughters—the time I spend with the Lord is very different. Parenting, especially in the early years, requires us to have great grace as we struggle to find uninterrupted time to maintain consistent meeting times with the Lord.

That's why the season of being a parent of a baby or young child—and this is true for any particularly intense season of life—is a great time to practice the art of *paying attention.* With little ones to care for, you may not be able to sit down with a Bible every day. Maybe you can carve out time once a week—or maybe not. But you can still pay attention to what God is saying to you through other people, at church, in a Bible verse written on an index card that's taped to your bathroom mirror, and reading a one-page devotional as you wait for an appointment.

When you remember that God wants to speak to you, you are more likely to hear His voice. And when you hear His voice, you will hunger for more extended time with your Beloved.

Those "dates" will come, and when they do, they'll strengthen your relationship. But in between those times, look for ways—even small ways—to connect with the Lord. (He loves it when you check in with Him!)

One more thing. Sharing with your kids how you are paying attention to God's presence in your life and what you are seeing can also be very faith-building—for them as well as for you. When we talk about this on a regular basis, children begin to share their own experiences with us and with one another.

Our oldest granddaughter, for instance, told us that a girl in her class had been removed from an extremely abusive situation and then adopted.

The other kids made fun of her because she was different and had a rash on her arm. Our granddaughter asked her if she knew Jesus and told her how He would be with her and help her. That story helped build up my granddaughter's faith—and it also built up mine.

Snapshot III – Then there were those seasons, sometimes dictated by a change in job, when I walked on a treadmill in the morning, and that's where I prayed, listened to hymns or praise music, read Scripture verse cards, or read an inspirational book.

Snapshot IV – These days, any seat where I have my computer or iPad is my sacred spot for having devotions and reading the Bible on BibleGateway.com. (This website also has email devotions, newsletters, and a Verse of the Day.) Often when I finish my devotions, I find myself wishing I could stay longer in God's sweet presence. My husband, Ron, settles into an overstuffed chair in the bedroom for his devotional times. Since he is blind, he listens to the Bible on tape or Christian programs on TV.

Snapshot V – As I mentioned earlier, I've occasionally had a half-day or full-day retreat for spiritual renewal, and those times enriched my relationship with the Lord. I've also gone on some two- or three-day retreats alone. During those retreats, when I read and reflected on Scripture, reassessed the course of my life, and sought spiritual refreshment. Experiencing the life-changing presence of God at times like these fueled my desire to be with Him. Retreats aren't a possibility for me in this season of life as I care for my husband and granddaughters, but that season may return.

As these snapshots of my life show, our time with God changes as our circumstances do, and as our personal and spiritual needs change, so may our times with the Lord. The Lord knows best what we need for our spiritual growth and what we need to learn in order to be His servant. Of course our needs will be different from others. How the Lord guides us—what book or music or person or passage of Scripture He uses in our lives—changes as we move through life.

The truth is, each one of us is in a stage of our sacred journey that we've never been on before. Maybe this stage calls us to scale mountainsides, maybe we find ourselves in a dry, dangerous desert, or maybe we're enjoying gentle winds blowing through a lush countryside. Whatever the terrain, we have no idea what divine appointments—either delightful serendipities or sudden challenges—await us.

After my husband became blind and we found ourselves dealing with a series of intense health issues and family trials, I drew away from God—yet at the same time I yearned for Him and sought Him.

I was on a spiritual seesaw, longing for God even as I angrily accused Him of failing us. Only rarely did I set aside time to be alone with Him.

It took me years to regain spiritual stability, and I discovered through it all that God was seeking *me* and working in my life in ways I would never have chosen. He was teaching me life-changing and liberating truth about His Sovereignty and what He wanted for my life.

Clearly, God's ways of training us are not our ways. His ways of growing our faith are not ours. We may not understand why God doesn't intervene, why we have to live with a chronic problem or unrelenting heartache. We may even give up spiritually because we feel abandoned or hopeless. Yet even "if we are faithless, he remains faithful" (2 Timothy 2:13 NIV).

In fact, often the hardest times in our lives help us turn to God simply to be with Him, not to get something from Him. And during those tough times, we learn that, no matter what we're thinking or feeling about Him and no matter what He's allowing to happen in our life, He is still turned toward us.

REMAINING IN THE VINE

Jesus is our model for living with a heart devoted to God, yet at first glance it doesn't seem that Jesus led a very disciplined life. He wandered from town to village, responding in the moment as He taught people, healed them, and delivered them from demons. But we need to realize that everywhere Jesus went, every miracle He performed, everything He ever did, He did because He was listening to and being led by His Father.

Henri Nouwen said it this way: "Jesus is not only our Savior simply because of what he said to us or did for us. He is our Savior because what he said and did was said and done in obedience to his Father."[16]

Through His single-minded obedience to God, Jesus showed us what it means to lead a life devoted to following God. Nouwen continued: "[Jesus's] obedience means a total, fearless listening to his loving Father. Between the Father and the Son there is only love. . . . It is a caring, yet demanding love. It is a supportive, yet severe love. It is a gentle, yet strong love. It is a love that gives life, yet accepts death. In this divine love Jesus was sent into the world; to this divine love Jesus offered himself on the cross."[17]

Jesus not only submitted Himself to the demands of God's holy love, but He also demonstrated what it means to be perfected in suffering:

"Although he was a son, he learned obedience from what he suffered and, once made perfect, he became the source of eternal salvation for all who obey him" (Hebrews 5:8-9).

Jesus showed us how we're to live out our faith and draw ever closer to the Lover of our soul. Jesus did nothing apart from God's guidance or outside of His power, and neither can we. Jesus did everything in accordance with His Father's will, and so must we. Jesus learned obedience through suffering, and so can we. Jesus remained in His Father's love by spending hours alone with Him. He often withdrew to lonely places and prayed (Luke 5:16).

The disciple Mark reported the same about our Lord: "Very early in the morning, while it was still dark, Jesus got up, left the house and went off to a solitary place, where he prayed" (Mark 1:35).

As we seek times and places to be with God in different seasons of our life, our ultimate goal is to remain in Christ the Vine. Our Creator is the Master Gardener who desires to plant His Word in our heart and bring it to fruition in our life. And this Master Gardener calls us to cling to the Vine even in harsh conditions because that is how new, sweet life will come.

Seeking after God in every season of life will allow Him to cultivate the soil of our hearts, prune sin, cut off dead branches, and tenderly nurture our growth. He yearns to meet with us in a simple, sacred place where we can flourish in His watchful, protecting presence.

✧ *Prayer* ✧

Lord God, I call to You. Evening, morning, and noon. I cry out in distress, and You hear my voice . . . I cast all my cares on You, for You never let the righteous fall . . . Your steadfast love never ceases; Your mercies never come to an end; they are new every morning; great is Your faithfulness. "The Lord is my portion," says my soul, "therefore I will hope in him." . . . You are good to me when I wait for You and seek You with all my heart and soul . . . Who may ascend Your hill, O Lord? Who may stand in Your holy place? . . . Where will wisdom be found? And where is the place of understanding? You understand the way to it, and You know its place. Lord, to fear You is wisdom, and to depart from evil is understanding. Show me the place where I can meet with You, where I can find Your wisdom and understanding . . . For You have promised to lead me in the way of wisdom and along straight paths.

—Psalm 55:16-17; 55:22; Lamentations 3:22-25; Jeremiah
29:13; Psalm 24:3; Job 28:12, 23, 28 rsv; Proverbs 4:11

✣ Practicing the Spiritual Life ✣

1. Why is it significant that God watches over you as a vinedresser watches over his vines? What impact does this knowledge have on your desire to know God better?

2. What area of your life, if any, have you cut off from the Vine? Why—and what have been the consequences of doing so? In what specific areas would you like the Lord to strengthen your attachment to Him?

3. Meeting faithfully with the Lord when we experience opposition is difficult. Opposition may come from others, but it may also come from our own nature or a demanding work schedule. If you struggle to meet regularly with the Lord, ask Him to show you how you can consistently meet with Him despite conflicts and demands. If you have an established pattern of meeting with God already, what changes, if any, do you feel impressed to make as a result of reading this chapter?

4. To follow Christ's example, we need to think of creative ways to be with Him. For starters, set a specific date and hour to spend a longer period of time with Him. Write this appointment on your calendar. This one hour can make a huge difference in strengthening your relationship with God. The impact of a half-day or full-day retreat can be even greater.

CHAPTER 8

KEEP A SPIRITUAL JOURNAL

Let love and faithfulness never leave you;
bind them around your neck,
write them on the tablet of your heart.

—*Proverbs 3:3*

As we travel along on our spiritual journey, we may not see the connection between those harsh stretches and what seems to be God's slowness in answering or intervening. Years later, however, we can look back and realize how—even when we couldn't see it—He was making circumstances in our lives work together according to His plans.

A spiritual journal is a tool that can help us discover those connections, to see the fingerprints of our loving God when He seemed so far way. Our journals enable us to go back and see where we have been, recognize that God was right there with us all the time, and be reminded of where we're headed. Reviewing our journey helps us recall the places where we stopped, times we wandered, the scenery along the route, and how far we've traveled.

THE VALUE OF A JOURNAL

A spiritual journal is meant to be private, a place for us to record our struggles and our insights, our hopes and our hurts, our thoughts and our questions about our personal and spiritual life. We don't write a journal to impress anyone; we write for God and for ourselves.

Although keeping a spiritual journal can help us learn about ourselves, this is not its main focus. Our purpose is to find out more about God and what He desires of us. One faithful journal keeper wrote, "If a journal answers just one question, it is: What is God doing in my life?"[18]

Throughout the year, I reflect on Scriptures or insights from devotional books, and then I respond in my journal. By listening to Scriptures, waiting for the Lord to impress His desires on my mind, and then recording my responses on paper, I begin to see how the Lord is directing me. Furthermore, my thoughts remain more tuned to His still, small voice when I regularly read the Bible or other Christian books, when I at the same time write out what I learn and seek His guidance.

Writing in a journal helps me concentrate on personal and spiritual needs, express my fears and worries, and gain a clearer sense of God's direction for me. A journal also gives me a record of my life that I can read again. I've noticed, sadly, that when I don't write at all, I almost immediately forget what the Spirit of God impresses on me during my reading and prayer time.

Although journal writing is valuable for developing our spiritual life, it doesn't need to be an obligation. I don't write in my journal every day. Instead, I write when I feel inspired or I've gained a special insight. I write when I need to express my feelings about certain issues that I am working through. I write when I'm experiencing difficult trials and don't know what to do. I write when problems grow worse and no solution seems near.

No wonder my journal is especially comforting in times of grief and heartache. I look back and see that expressing my cares, fears, and worries on paper helped me identify my concerns. I realize that when I searched for verses and asked God to give me comfort, direction, and support through His Word, He did. This record of God's faithfulness encourages me to seek His wisdom and His spiritual principles that I can apply to my real-life situations.

Yet if I only wrote about my trials, I would remain in bondage to them. When I put my concerns and requests on paper and include relevant Scripture, hymns, or quotes from other inspirational books, I gain spiritual balance. I receive God's healing encouragement through His Word: the truths of Scripture help me release the pain, gain a godly and eternal perspective, and release the situation into His good and perfect care.

Periodically I go back and read over my journal entries. As I do, I note in the margins how God has answered prayer or helped me resolve a problem. Often I wonder why I was so anxious about certain situations. God brought me through: why had I been so worried? Other points in the journal remind me of long-term prayer requests that I still hope God will answer. Most importantly, though, my journals speak loudly of God's great faithfulness.

Rueben P. Job mentions yet another benefit of keeping a journal: "I have often been surprised at how I have been helped and healed by putting in writing my thoughts, prayers, questions, and responses to life. I have been even more surprised to find God's message for me in what I had written a month, year, or ten years earlier."[19]

As a result of our pastor's suggestion, I also started recording answered prayers in a blank book. That experience taught me more about prayer—both the joyous surprises and the unexpected disappointments. I've even written down what appeared to be final answers only to have them turn into shocking reversals.

Keeping a record of answered prayers has strengthened my faith. God has answered faithfully—from giving my husband and me strength to complete difficult work projects, to providing me with a new teaching job in the town we moved to, to starting a ministry that I'd desired for a long time.

A GUIDE FOR JOURNAL WRITING

Some people use a blank book or small loose-leaf notebook for journaling. I usually journal on a computer because that's where I do all of my writing.

But words aren't the only way to journal. You might enjoy drawing pictures or sketches in your journal, making brief notes of their significance. You don't need to be an artist; your pictures can be as simple as a child's stick figures.

You may also enjoy doing calligraphy to record Scriptures, prayers, or spiritual insights. If you don't like writing, you could also speak into a digital recorder and make an audio journal.

Here are a few other suggestions to help you get started:

1. *Write the time, day, and date at the top of the page.* After you finish the entry, you may want to go back and add a title that summarizes your thoughts or concerns. Later, when you want to reread a particu-

lar entry, the title helps you find what you're looking for, and the date gives you a context.

2. *Don't worry about how much you write.* You'll probably write more on some days than on others. You may write very little while other people fill volumes. You don't have to meet any standards: you aren't going to be critiqued or graded. You're not writing for publication, so don't be overly concerned about grammar, punctuation, and spelling—and feel free to develop your own shorthand. If you journal on the computer, let your thoughts flow without correcting what you write. When you finish, you can always use the spell checker if you want to.

3. *Write without self-editing or censoring your thoughts.* Don't allow your inner critic to shame you, cause you to feel embarrassed, or keep you from writing whatever is on your heart and mind.

4. *If your thoughts wander, write those thoughts down too.* And if all you can think about is what you need to accomplish, stop, make a "to do" list, and then set it aside. After you do that, you'll probably find it much easier to focus on the Lord.

Once you start your journal, keep these ideas in mind:

As you write your thoughts and even read them later, try to achieve a balanced, godly perspective by seeking out and including God's views. I realize a journal is a place to be reflective, but it may also be used to study a Bible passage.

Record Bible verses, quotes from books, or ideas from online sermons or podcasts that especially convict you or minister to you.

A Bible index or concordance can be a valuable help. I use *Strong's*

Exhaustive Concordance of the Bible and the *New International Version of the Thompson Chain-Reference Bible* to look up specific verses and topics. Then I meditate on what I have learned during my study and how the Scripture speaks to me.

When recording Scripture passages or quotes from other books in your journal, include the chapter and verses and/or the author and title. Then say why the verses or quotes are significant to you: what is happening in your life, what concerns you, and what about that passage was helpful.

When I read over my writings later, I find I've usually forgotten about a difficult day. It seems so different in light of where my life is months or years afterward. I may wonder why I was so worried, or I may feel grateful that God graciously brought me through such a painful time.

Write about what is happening in your life that day. Ask the Lord questions about how to deal with any person, problem, or situation that troubles you, and listen for His answers, guidance, and comforting words.

That said, keep in mind this truth: "Journaling does not satisfy all our queries. We may leave our journals filled with unanswered questions—Can we? Will we? When will God . . . ? A lack of closure prods us to continue the listening awareness. . . . After days or weeks or months, we are prepared to hear fragments of answers that emerge in the encouragement of a friend or the confrontation of a co-worker. In the meantime, we have learned to rest and listen even though life is full of ferment."[20]

Be honest. Express your true feelings—your anger, anxiety, fears, grief— as freely as you do your appreciation, joy, and praise. Write down even those struggles that seem trivial. Recording your inner conflicts puts a name to them and frees you to address the real issues.

Write freely as ideas come and without thinking too much about what you're saying. Writing without putting limits on what you say or how you say it is an excellent way to gain insights into your true self, insights you may feel uncomfortable with or even dislike. When you're willing to be transparent, you'll see yourself in ways you never have before.

If you're still hesitant, consider this about the Psalms: "David's hard honesty reveals that journaling is a place to be our true selves and to offer our true, sometimes unflattering views. . . . David moved from revenge to hopelessness to praise."[21]

Confess your sins and repent so that the Lord may transform you. You don't need to be afraid to ask the Lord to reveal whatever He desires you to see about your real self. How can you receive God's transforming love if you reject yourself? And if you reject God's convicting love as well, how can you cooperate with Him and be changed into His likeness?

So ask the Lord to help you have His thoughts about yourself as well as about your circumstances and relationships. Ask for deliverance from angry, bitter, and/or unbalanced attitudes. Ask Him to help you take responsibility for ways you have contributed to your problems or strained relationships. What do you need to change about the way you think and act?

Rather than rejecting yourself because you feel inferior, unworthy, or ashamed of what you see in yourself, be open to what God is trying to show you. If pride and self-delusion are keeping you from seeing your true self, ask God to reveal truth to you. He will be gentle: He will reveal only what you are able to deal with at this point.

When He does help you see yourself more accurately, confess your sins in a written prayer. When you see your sins in ink, they become real; you cannot think or wish them away. As an act of cleansing and repentance, make a covenant with the Lord to turn away from those wrongs—and make restitution where possible.

Maybe you have painful secrets. If so, you'll find it helps to write about them. They may be secrets about yourself or others, and carrying them all on your own has been a burden. If you're writing about personal sins or secrets, search for Scriptures to help you work through the process of embracing God's forgiveness and experiencing the personal and spiritual restoration He wants you to know.

Lean on the Holy Spirit and Scripture for truth and for strength. God's Spirit and His written Word help us overcome sin, release us from shame, and provide the support we need to change and grow.

Then make a ceremony of tearing up or even burning your written confessions. Doing so will help free you from the bondage of guilt and remind you that the Lord bore all your sins and burdens on the cross. You don't have to bear them any longer.

Next, commit yourself to being accountable to God and to another trustworthy Christian of the same sex. If you feel the Lord prompting you to do so, confess to that person or to a Christian counselor or pastor the sin you're finding hard to release. Spoken confession shines light into the darkness, keeps it from remaining hidden, and helps break the power it has over us.

Throughout this entire process, remember that "the LORD is gracious and compassionate, slow to anger and rich in love. The LORD is good to all; he has compassion on all he has made" (Psalm 145:8-9).

Though it's humbling and difficult, I've gone through this journaling and confession process many times and always found in it healing, hope, a renewed connection with my heavenly Father, and new growth.

One experience in particular changed my life. Convicted by the Holy Spirit, I realized that I was constantly complaining to others just as the Israelites had murmured bitterly against Moses and God as they traveled through the desert.

I also realized that I didn't trust my Lord during tough times due to this complaining that kept me focused on circumstances rather than on Him. These passages especially convicted me: "Now the people complained about their hardships in the hearing of the LORD, and when he heard them his anger was aroused . . . The LORD said to Moses, 'How long will these people treat me with contempt? How long will they refuse to believe in me, in spite of all the miraculous signs I have performed among them?'" (Numbers 11:1; 14:11).

I recognized that even though I was encountering many trials, God expected me to trust Him no matter what went wrong. He helped me see that my grumbling was only making me more anxious and afraid. I needed to change my attitude and choose to express my trust in God. I needed to be grateful for all the wondrous ways He had led me up to this point and answered my heart cries along the way.

I still pour out my grief and heartaches to the Lord in my journal; He wants us to do so. But to maintain and sometimes to even gain a spiritual perspective, I write Scripture passages, prayers, and praises that affirm His abiding presence and faithfulness in all circumstances.

Finally, praise God and express your gratitude for the specific things He has accomplished for you. Worship God simply for who He is. Your spirit will be lifted and your heart encouraged when you rejoice in the Lord's goodness, grace, and kindness. Then review the many ways He has provided, protected, and blessed you. Your faith in His faithfulness will be reinforced.

A spiritual journal helps us see the growth in our lives. When we read back over our writings, we can see when the roses blossomed, those moments when God's grace was magnificently on display. We may also see that, during trials, our peace wilted like rose petals in the scorching heat. Maybe our faith was pruned until nothing remained but thorny sticks locked in the hardened earth. When that desolate season finally ended, however, we again saw fresh, green shoots of faith and hope springing forth.

Be encouraged as you journal and then when you go back to read your journals, you'll recognize more clearly what the Lord is accomplishing in your life. You'll become aware of spiritual growth and maturity. You'll find yourself drawn closer and closer to your Lord, and you'll see Him in ways you never have before.

✌ *Prayer* ✎

May your love and faithfulness never leave me, God. I want to bind them around my neck, write them on the tablet of my heart . . . "Teach me your way, O Lord, and I will walk in your truth; give me an undivided heart, that I may fear your name." . . . "Test me, O Lord, and try me, examine my heart and my mind; for your love is ever before me." Teach me how to walk continually in Your truth.

—Proverbs 3:3; Psalm 86:11; 26:2–3

✌ *Practicing the Spiritual Life* ✎

1. Have you ever kept a journal of any kind? What do you see as the difference between a spiritual journal and a daily journal of activities and thoughts? What is the benefit of each?

2. What are your feelings about keeping a spiritual journal? Excitement? Guilt? Fear? Curiosity? Why?

3. When have you learned something about yourself or your relationship with God from journaling about an experience or memorializing it in some way?

4. What other creative ways besides journaling could you use to record God's faithfulness? Could a rock or a bench serve as a memorial? What about a quilt or a painting?

5. To start or even add to a spiritual journal, try this exercise: List a few significant "firsts" in your life—your first job, your first breakup, your first experience with injustice, your first loss of a loved one. Next to each, note a characteristic of God that you experienced in each of those firsts.

CHAPTER 9

*PLANT THE WORD
IN YOUR MIND
AND HEART*

*Oh, the joys of those who do not follow the advice of the wicked,
or stand around with sinners, or join in with mockers.
But they delight in the law of the LORD, meditating on it day and night.
They are like trees planted along the riverbank, bearing fruit each season.
Their leaves never wither, and they prosper in all they do.*

—*Psalm 1:1-3,* NLT

Whether we're awake or asleep, the information our brain is sending and receiving at any moment could overwhelm a telephone system!

Our mind is like the volumes of an encyclopedia that store a wide variety of subject matter. Our memory, however, is selective. My husband, for instance, can chart the history of our married life by the cars we have owned—but I couldn't even tell you the make or model of the last car we had. And how many of us have memorized information for an exam and then immediately forgotten it once the test was over?

This selective nature of our memory impacts learning Scripture. A few people may be able to recall hundreds of Bible passages, but most of us need to be intentional about memorizing verses. It's not something that comes easily to me, but I've found that the blessings of Scripture memorization are well worth the effort.

WHY MEMORIZE SCRIPTURE?

First, memorizing Scripture is valuable because repeating a verse again and again in order to memorize it makes its meaning more personal and more real. And of course it does, "for the word of God is living and active, sharper than any two-edged sword, piercing to the division of soul and of spirit, of joints and of marrow, and discerning the thoughts and intentions of the heart" (Hebrews 4:12 ESV).

Similarly, when a verse of Scripture or a song we sang in church plays over and over in my mind later, I stop and ask the Lord what He's trying to say to me. Other times I realize it's His way of keeping my thoughts tuned to His presence. Then, as I meditate on His Word, God opens my heart to know more of His character and His sovereignty.

Another reason to memorize God's Word is because it truly is soul food: His truth nourishes our spirit. We come away from the table of Scripture full and satisfied. Later, when we are thirsty and hungry and needy, God brings to mind what we have memorized, and we again feel fed. Our faith is energized again and again from the nutrients of the Word that we have hidden in our heart.

Most important of all, memorizing Scripture helps us keep our thoughts on the Lord all the time.

HOW TO MEMORIZE SCRIPTURE

How do we memorize Scripture? One of the greatest helps in memorizing is to know how we assimilate information. Everyone has a dominant learning style, be it auditory, visual, or tactile-kinesthetic.

If you're an auditory learner, you learn best by listening to a speaker or hearing music. You probably remember songs better than something you read. Learning Scripture songs is a great way for auditory learners to memorize God's Word.

If you're a visual learner, you gain more information from seeing illustrations and a chart or diagram than from reading words without pictures. So when you memorize Scripture, you might imagine an actual cross if the word *cross* is in the verse, or you may picture the words of a verse on the page.

If you're a tactile-kinesthetic learner (I am), you need to see how something is done: you learn best when you can feel, touch, and do things with your hands. For example, I enjoy using a computer, but I have a difficult time learning new software programs by just reading an instruction manual. I learn best when I can watch someone demonstrate procedures and then practice them at the same time.

Everyone uses all three learning styles, but one or two will be more dominant in each of us. So, whether you are an auditory, visual, or tactile-kinesthetic learner, here are some methods to help you learn Scripture.

Using all of the following ways to learn a verse or passage would be too confusing. Simply try different ideas until you find the ones that work well for you.

IDEAS FOR MEMORIZING SCRIPTURE

Learn Scriptures that fit your circumstances or express your own feelings. When I have a particular concern or am going through a trial, learning verses that apply to those situations serves as a constant reminder of God's caring presence. Or if I'm struggling with a sin in my life, I concentrate on verses that help me work on overcoming it.

Write or type the Scripture verse on several index cards. Put one card by your bed with your devotional materials, one in your car, one where you eat, and one at work so you can practice learning the verse throughout the day. If you like to walk or ride a stationary bicycle, you can work on memorizing Scripture as you exercise.

You might also want to share the blessings by sharing with others copies of the verses you memorize. My friend Carolyn chose to learn Psalm 121, and she wrote out several copies on floral stationery. Then she sent them to friends.

One mutual friend told me she was extremely ill and going through other difficult trials and had asked the Lord to send her encouragement. The next day she received the handwritten psalm. She felt the Lord had sent her the encouragement she had prayed for. I was also greatly comforted when Carolyn gave a copy of the psalm to me because at the time I was facing major changes in my life.

Look for word patterns and/or focus on certain words. For example, underline the first couple of words of each sentence and any words that are repeated. Emphasize those underlined words when you say them out loud so you can set the pattern in your mind. Use those words as memorization cues. For example, note in Psalm 119:16-17 the repetition and the emphasis on *I will* and *word*: "I delight in your decrees; I *will* not neglect your *word*. Do good to your servant, and I *will* live; I *will* obey your *word*." If you remember the opening word of a phrase or sentence or words that are repeated, you'll find it much easier to learn the rest of the verse.

Memorize a phrase at a time. Say the first phrase five to ten times, emphasizing key words. Repeat the first and second phrases together the same number of times. Keep adding and repeating more phrases in that manner. Finally, repeat the whole verse aloud ten times or more. You can avoid rote memorization of the verse by thinking about its meaning as you learn it.

Keep your thoughts focused on the verse. Many of us struggle with meandering thoughts. It may encourage you to realize that most of us have to keep disciplining our minds when we're trying to memorize a verse. Our mind wanders from one concern or duty to the next. When that happens to me, I sometimes hold out my hand as if it's a stop sign to help me refocus my thoughts on the verse. Also, repeat the verse out loud to keep your thoughts on it. Run your finger along the words to hold your attention as you read it aloud.

Meditate on the Scripture that you're learning. Charles Stanley talked about the value of doing so: "I have come to realize that my thirst is quenched as I spend time meditating on the Word of God. Meditation is not mystical. Rather, it is the extremely practical and nourishing exercise of pondering and thinking on what God is saying through His Word. It is the art of asking questions of the Scriptures and then of yourself and discovering how the truth examined can be applied to your life and the particular problems you face."[22]

As I meditate on the Word and seek the Lord's thoughts, He speaks to me in many ways. He comforts, convicts, and counsels me.

He delivers me from sin and distorted thinking, and I continue to develop a deeper, stronger relationship with Him.

Learn Scripture songs. If you enjoy singing, one of the easiest ways to memorize the Bible is to learn Scripture choruses. I enjoy singing Scripture more than just saying it, and I remember those verses longer because I associate the words with music.

Take plenty of time to learn Scripture. The length of time to memorize a verse or passage isn't important. I've spent several weeks and sometimes even months learning passages.

Keep reviewing the passage once you've learned it. Repeating a verse helps us retain it. If we haven't practiced the verse for a day or two, we may be able to repeat most of it if we just glance at the first few words. Once we stop going over the verse, it easily slips out of our memory. But know that it's much easier to relearn a passage that you've previously memorized than it was to learn it initially.

CASE IN POINT:
COLOSSIANS 3:15-16

Let's look at how to use specific strategies to memorize this passage from Colossians: "Let the peace of Christ rule in your hearts, since as members of one body you were called to peace. And be thankful. Let the word of Christ dwell in you richly as you teach and admonish one another with all wisdom, and as you sing psalms, hymns and spiritual songs with gratitude in your hearts to God" (3:15-16).

Use hand gestures or sign language. Signing is a great way to reinforce a verse in your mind. Use American Sign Language or make up your own hand gestures. Consider, for example, "Let the peace of Christ rule in your hearts." *Let* means "to allow to pass," so make a gesture as if you're allowing someone to pass by. For *peace* use the peace sign. For *rule* pretend you're holding a ruler. For *hearts* draw the shape in the air or place your hand on your chest.

Associate words with mental pictures of certain things or people. Let the word *peace* prompt a picture of a dove; *Christ*, a familiar painting of Him; *rule*, a measuring stick; *hearts*, red hearts; *members*, specific people at church; and *word*, a Bible.

Do a study of key words. We learn verses more easily when we understand their meaning. The passage also becomes more personal, touching our heart in a deeper way and giving us greater insight into the richness of Scripture. Study the passage in several different versions of the Bible and various commentaries. Look up key words from the Old Testament in Hebrew using *Nelson's Expository Dictionary of the Old Testament*. For New Testament words in the Greek, use *An Expository Dictionary of New Testament Words* by W. E. Vine. *Strong's Exhaustive Concordance of the Bible* has both Hebrew and Greek dictionaries.

Consider, for instance, what *peace* and *rule* mean in "Let the *peace* of God *rule* in your heart, since as members of one body you were called to peace." The Greek word for peace means "quietness; rest; to set at one again"; it also means "to have harmonious relationships." *Rule* means "to arbitrate or act as an umpire or referee."

Paraphrase the passage. Once you've studied the meaning of the words, paraphrase the verses or make up Scripture prayers to further cement your understanding. Here's what you could do with verse 15: "May the quietness and rest that come with peace help me to be at peace with others. May peace be like an umpire that rules my heart with fairness so that I work well with the other members of the team that is the body of Christ."

Learn the Word to help you with everyday needs and in times of stress. Several years ago I went through a frightening time when my throat sometimes went into spasms and restricted my air passage and ability to swallow. I felt as if I were being strangled.

During one of these times, I was making a frantic drive to the doctor's office. I kept praying: I'd inhale with "Let the peace of Christ" and then I'd exhale with "rule in my heart." I kept repeating the phrase to calm myself and keep my blood pressure from soaring, which it had done during earlier attacks.

I prayed that verse over and over again during the following weeks as my throat continued to close up, as I went to several specialists, and as I underwent a traumatic regimen of tests, x-rays, and a misdiagnosis. I eventually found out that a chronic dry throat from using a breathing machine at night for a sleep disorder was causing the spasms.

When x-rays showed that I had nose and throat obstructions, I was grateful that the problem could be relieved without surgery. The most comforting discovery, however, was that repeating this verse enabled me to let Christ's peace rule my heart and mind and gave me the courage to endure a terrifying time.

Learn the Word in order to live by it. Be gentle on yourself if, like me, you don't have the gift of memorization. Again, the point is not how many verses we can quote. God desires that we implant His Word in our minds and hearts so we can apply it to how we live. God's greatest pleasure is seeing the transforming power of His Word change us into His likeness.

ᜤ *Prayer* ᜤ

O Lord, put Your law in my mind and write it on my heart . . . For Your Word is "living and active. Sharper than any double-edged sword, it penetrates even to dividing soul and spirit, joints and marrow; it judges the thoughts and attitudes of [my] heart." Nothing in all creation is hidden from Your sight. Everything is uncovered and laid bare before You . . . "Praise be to you, O LORD; teach me your decrees. With my lips I recount all the laws that come from your mouth. I rejoice in following your statutes as one rejoices in great riches. I meditate on your precepts and consider your ways. I delight in your decrees; I will not neglect your word."
. . . By Your grace, I will share Your Word at home, when I walk along the road, when I lie down, and when I get up . . . When Your words come, I will eat them; they are my joy and my heart's delight, for I bear Your name, O LORD God Almighty.

—Jeremiah 31:33; Hebrews 4:12–13; Psalm 119:12–
16; Deuteronomy 6:7; Jeremiah 15:16

ᜤ *Practicing the Spiritual Life* ᜤ

1. What would you say is your primary learning style: auditory, visual, or tactile-kinesthetic?

2. Explain the difference between rote memorization and meaningful memorization.

3. Why can having God's Word *in* us transform us?

4. Choose one verse to memorize this week and then use one or two of this chapter's ideas for memorizing God's Word.

Part Three

~

THE

PRAYING

LIFE

CHAPTER 10

SIMPLE PRAYER

The world is full of so-called prayer warriors who are prayer-ignorant.
They're full of formulas and programs and advice, peddling techniques for
getting what you want from God. Don't fall for that nonsense. This is your
Father you are dealing with, and he knows better than you what you need.
With a God like this loving you, you can pray very simply.

—Matthew 6:7-9, MSG

A few years ago I was in a women's group, and we were discussing why we didn't pray more. One woman shared that a woman in their church had started an intercessory group—and no one went. Another woman, a mother of five and caretaker for her own mother, said, "Sometimes I think God doesn't see what I have to do in a day. If He only knew, He'd understand why I don't have time to pray. Of course, I know He knows." Then she suggested, "Maybe we could try praying for two minutes at a time throughout the day."

We talked about not having enough time to pray now, but thought that perhaps we would spend hours in prayer when we were older and had more time. But *will* we have more time? I'm seventy-four years old now, and I work harder and have heavier obligations than I did when I was younger. Having more time to pray hasn't come to me yet!

What freed me to pray was my discovery of two things: first, prayer begins not with us, but with God. Second, prayer is simple.

PRAYER BEGINS WITH GOD

Isn't prayer *our* responsibility? And shouldn't we be praying all the time? The truth is, I often forget to pray, and often I don't pray very long. So, for years, I felt like a failure in this area of my spiritual life. It helps me to remember that God created prayer and that prayer begins with Him. His Spirit is speaking to mine all the time. He calls me to respond, through my prayers, to the impressions He lays upon my heart.

How does the Spirit of God speak to us and help us pray? His Spirit prompts us about very practical things we may need to do or say. He convicts us of attitudes that need changing and actions we need to stop doing. He urges us to serve our family or meet a need for strangers.

The difficulty with prayer is that God does not communicate with us in the same way we communicate with people. We can't have face-to-face, back-and-forth conversations with the Lord as we do with our loved ones. We can't see God's face or hold His hand or hug Him. Prayer is not even like talking on the phone because we can't hear His voice audibly.

In addition to those impediments to prayer, you may also be wary about hearing God speak because of the exaggerated claims of people who say God has spoken to them when they are clearly trying to manipulate you to do something for them or to give money to their ministry. Maybe such a charlatan has taken advantage of you in the past.

So how *do* you discern when God is speaking to you? You need to know Jesus Christ as your Savior, and His Spirit will help you distinguish between the truth of the Word of God and false teaching about Him. You learn the truths of the Bible by reading and studying it, praying for discernment, and hearing the Gospel preached and taught.

God's directions are usually clear, direct, and simple. He will not lie to you or lead you in the wrong direction. He is the only One who fully knows you and your needs because He is the only One who is with you twenty-four hours a day, seven days a week.

To hear God, we need to open our hearts to what He is saying to us through Scripture. Let us consider this caution: If we only listen for what we want God to say, if we only watch for what we want Him to do, or if we stay focused on ourselves as we ask for what we need, we become deaf to what He is saying to us. He makes His presence known to us when we truly listen. The Spirit repeats His directions, and when we need to respond immediately, His encouragement to act grows stronger and stronger.

Listening and watching for the Spirit's guidance grows our faith and deepens our relationship with God, and of course this growth is a process that takes time. As we act on our desire to be more aware of God's presence and instructions, He responds and enables us to start recognizing when He is speaking to us as well as the ways He reveals Himself and His plans to us. The Lord wants us to know Him, to speak to Him, and to listen to Him. That's why He always makes the first move and comes to us. God carries the burden of prayer for us; our part is to listen for His guidance and then respond in obedience.

LANA'S PRAYER

The following story illustrates what I mean about how prayer begins with God and how the Spirit can prompt us to act even when we are unaware of His presence with us at the moment or His involvement in our current life situation.

One morning a few years ago, my friend Lana started her day by praying, "Lord, direct my day and show me what You want me to do."

That same morning I had an appointment for a mammogram. My regular doctor had recommended it because I had a breast infection with a lump and a large area that was fiery red. Every bone in my body ached.

The doctor ruled out a boil, but she didn't rule out my greatest fear. The worst word out of her mouth was the *C* word. I'd had surgery on my right breast a few years earlier to remove cancer. Since then I had been cancer-free, but the possibility of that deadly disease's return had continued to concern me. I was scared because I was so sick, and the antibiotics weren't touching the infection or easing the pain in my bones.

Wednesday, the day before the mammogram, I was thinking about what I would do if I had cancer, especially if it had already spread throughout my body. With Ron being blind, how would we manage? I was depressed, exhausted, sick, and feeling deeply sorry for myself. I didn't want to face the mammogram alone, but I am not one to call a friend to ask her to go along with me.

That same day, my friend Dixie felt impressed to email me and ask how I was doing. She didn't even know about the infection or the cancer scare until I emailed her back and told her. Dixie's husband, Greg, has been a caring pastor to us, and Ron attends a men's Bible study he leads in their garage. Greg has called on us many times and prayed with us, especially during the long hard years our son and his wife were waiting to see if they could adopt our three granddaughters.

Thursday morning, at 7:15 a.m., Greg called and wanted to pray with me before the test. As he prayed for my healing, he quoted Isaiah 65:24, "It shall come to pass that before they call, I will answer; and while they are still speaking, I will hear" (NKJV).

I was so thankful for his call and his prayers.

The mammogram was scheduled for 11:00 a.m., so I first went to the fabric store to buy some yardage I needed. When I walked into the fabric section, there was my friend Lana. She was thinking about making a quilt, but she didn't have anything definite in mind.

I was thrilled to see her. We chatted for a few minutes to catch up, and I told her about what was going on. I finished buying my fabric, and she walked me to the car. As I started to drive away, she ran back to the car and asked me, "Would you like me to go with you to your mammogram?"

I started to say no, but then I blurted out, "I would love to have you come with me!"

And what a comfort she was! I was so relieved that I didn't have to be alone as I waited for the test. Although I hadn't asked God to send a friend to go with me, He had known my heart cries.

After the test was over, I felt more than a little apprehensive as I waited for the results. Once again, I was so relieved to not be waiting alone.

When the doctor came in the room and started to speak, I couldn't take in all that he said. He had to tell me twice, "You do not have cancer. There is hardly any sign of an infection. Come back for your next mammogram in a year."

I was overjoyed. No sign of cancer! God had answered before we called on Him and had healed me as Greg prayed. We don't know what caused the infection, but we did know it was completely healed.

Lana and I went out to lunch together to celebrate the good news. God had known she was the one to send to the fabric store for a divine appointment. She was exactly the dear friend I needed to be with me. Over lunch, we got caught up and talked about the many ways we could see God working in our lives. We also shared our concerns and supported one another—just what good friends need to do.

Another amazing part of the story is that Lana lives in Nipomo, a town north of Santa Maria that has a wonderful fabric store, and she later said that she considered going to that store or to other stores north of her, especially one that has excellent discounts on fabric. But that morning she felt impressed to drive south to Santa Maria, which really made no sense at all.

Here in Santa Maria, there are two fabric stores next door to each other. One is huge, and the other one is a craft store with a small fabric section. She went to the store with the small section, and that was exactly where God wanted her to be.

Lana and I were astounded by this divine appointment. God had been speaking to and guiding both of us even though we hadn't realized it. Lana simply prayed for direction that morning, something she normally does. God spoke to her heart to go to a fabric store that was not even in her own town. God impressed on me to go to the same store—and to do so before my test instead of afterward. God directed us to go to the same store at the same time because I needed a friend that day, and He wanted to show us both how much He cares about His children and how He carefully guides our steps.

SIMPLE PRAYER

In addition to learning that God initiates prayer, I discovered that prayer is simple; it is very doable. Richard Foster described simple prayer as "the most primary form of prayer" and noted that it is sometimes called the "Prayer of Beginning Again."[23] Rosalind Rinker offered this encouragement to pray: "The more natural the prayer, the more real [God] becomes. It has all been simplified for me to this extent: prayer is a dialogue between two persons who love each other."[24] This basic truth is the foundation on which to build our prayer life.

Simple prayer is basic requests, short and to the point. Prayer is simply talking to the Lord about our daily concerns. It's everyday talk, not flowery words or theological language that sounds superspiritual. Prayer is just being yourself and speaking to God the way you carry on conversations with your loved ones.

As Foster wrote, "There is no pretense in Simple Prayer. We do not pretend to be more holy, more pure, or more saintly than we actually are. We do not try to conceal our conflicting and contradictory motives from God—or ourselves."[25] Simple prayer is being as real and truthful and transparent with the Lord as we can be. We don't have to be afraid that the Lord will criticize or tune us out. We can talk to the Lord without thinking ahead of time about what we need to say in order to be sure He will hear us or to persuade Him to answer us.

Simple prayer is listening and responding to the Holy Spirit's promptings. Pause . . . and just ask yourself, "What does God want of me now?" Pause . . . and listen. The answer has been on your heart for a while. Think about what you've been putting off. What prompting has been unrelenting or even urgent? As soon as you act, the urging will disappear. Then listen again. What does God want you to do or say next?

Simple prayer is conversational. So—either literally or figuratively—curl up on a soft sofa for a leisurely chat. Then talk heart-to-heart with the beloved Friend who knows you better than anyone else does. Relax in God's presence and be yourself without any apology or explanation. Enjoy a mutual friendship with the Lord: He wants you to know Him intimately just as He knows you. As you pray, remember you are safe and secure; you can completely trust your Soul Friend and tell Him your greatest concerns, knowing He will keep your deepest confidences. You can also sit quietly with Him without trying to fill any silence.

Simple prayer is telling the truth to the Lord. If we lie as a habit, we will lie to God and ourselves and our prayers turn into foolish babbling. "The LORD is righteous in all his ways and kind in all his works. The LORD is near to all who call on him, to all who call on him in truth" (Psalm 145:17–18 ESV).

Simple prayer is a beggar's plea. When blind Bartimaeus was sitting by the roadside begging, he learned that Jesus was coming, so he began to shout, "Jesus, Son of David, have mercy on me!" The crowd rebuked Bartimaeus, but he shouted even louder until Jesus stopped.

"What do you want me to do for you?" Jesus asked him.

The blind man said, "Rabbi, I want to see."

"Go," said Jesus, "your faith has healed you" (Mark 10:46-52).

What a simple exchange between Bartimaeus and Jesus—and what a clear reminder that the Lord cares about our personal concerns. In fact, the psalmist often cried out for help: "Come quickly to help me, O Lord my Savior" (Psalm 38:22) and "Listen to my cry, for I am in desperate need" (Psalm 142:6).

Some Christians, however, feel that simple prayer is too self-centered, that asking, begging, and pleading is not pleasing to God. Foster disagrees: "What these people fail to see, however, is that Simple Prayer is necessary, even essential, to the spiritual life. The only way we move beyond 'self-centered prayer' (if indeed we ever do) is by going through it, not by making a detour around it."[26]

Simple prayer is an attitude of our heart that appeals to God's heart. Too many believers have the misconception that the longer and more eloquent the prayer, the more able we are to persuade God to do what we want Him to do. In his classic book, *Prayer*, O. Hallesby made this point: "Prayer is something deeper than words. It is present in the soul before it has been formulated in words. And it abides in the soul after the last words of prayer have passed over our lips ... Prayer is a definite attitude of our hearts toward God, an attitude which He in heaven immediately recognizes as prayer, as an appeal to His heart. Whether it takes the form of words or not, does not mean anything to God, only to ourselves."[27]

Simple prayer can be one word, such as "Jesus." Simple prayer can even be a passing thought about a need, for the Lord hears and knows everything on our hearts. "You know my every thought when far away. . . . You know what I am going to say even before I say it, LORD" (Psalm 139:2, 4 NLT1996). As Jesus taught, "Your Father knows what you need before you ask him" (Matthew 6:8).

Simple prayer can even be a conversation with someone about our prayer needs that the Lord overhears. "For where two or three gather in my name, there am I with them" (Matthew 18:20 NIV).

Simple prayer can be a moan or a wordless cry of the heart. After all, God sees our tears and hears our weeping: He knows our unspoken prayers. Remember the woman who had been subject to bleeding for twelve years? She came up behind Jesus and touched the hem of His cloak because she thought, "If I just touch his clothes, I will be healed" (Mark 5:28). She immediately stopped bleeding. Jesus felt power going out of Him and asked who had touched His clothes. She came forward and told Him that she had been healed.

"He said to her, 'Daughter, your faith has healed you. Go in peace and be freed from your suffering'" (Mark 5:34). Jesus knew her thoughts and responded even though she wasn't consciously praying to Him.

Let us be encouraged that Jesus knows our thoughts when we don't even think of ourselves as praying. He is aware of our every need, and He longs for us to watch and see how He is working in response.

Simple prayer can be offered anytime and anyplace. We can develop the habit of coming into the Lord's presence for a few moments at a time as we do regular tasks—as we wash dishes, do laundry, vacuum, or undertake any other routine household or gardening job that doesn't require much thinking. We can embrace each of those chores as an opportunity to offer simple prayers to our attentive and loving Father.

One more thing. Our morning coffee could become a time for prayer rather than reading the newspaper. We don't have to keep thinking that we have to squeeze into our day an extra minute to pray. We can pray as we work throughout the day.

A SIMPLE PRAYER ANSWERED

Three years ago the Lord answered a simple prayer . . .

It had been raining and windy most of the morning, and I knew it would be a chilly Santa Maria day. I got up at 6:30, showered and dressed, then went to help get my granddaughters off to school. It's always a race against the clock to get everyone to dress, eat, brush teeth, comb hair, and get their backpacks and lunches.

I got Grace out the door to catch her ride and then watched the other two girls until right before ten when I took Lauren to kindergarten and Molly to preschool and then went to a doctor's appointment. I was done by eleven.

I sat in the car for a few minutes to read—my respite from the insistent needs of my family and the phone and all the other tasks that call my name. It started to pour, a pounding rain that thundered and rattled, so I thought I'd better get home. I put my key in the ignition, but my car wouldn't start. I waited and tried again, but it still didn't start. I panicked after several more tries. I didn't have a working cell phone, so I went back to the doctor's office to use their phone.

I was told it would be a thirty-minute wait for an Automobile Club tow truck. Well, I've been stuck with a broken car many times, and the wait had been at least that long and often longer. I had only eaten a piece of toast for breakfast, but I am a diabetic, and I was starting to have a low blood-sugar attack. There was no place to eat close by.

Besides, it was pouring rain. And if the car had to be towed to the mechanic, how would I pick up the girls at school? I was also fearful about the cost of car repairs. I knew our bank account was depleted. I was feeling overwhelmed with worry. Finally, I simply prayed, "Lord, help me." It was a quick cry of the heart.

Within a few minutes, the tow truck arrived in the thundering rain. The driver reminded me that my front lights were on, a detail I had forgotten. The battery needed charging—and so did my faith. Within five minutes I was on my way, relieved that the car was fine and grateful that God had heard and responded to my simple prayer.

ᘜ *Prayer* ᘛ

Lord, I come to you as a child . . . I don't want my prayers to be full of formulas and programs and advice; I don't want to experiment with techniques for getting what I want from You. You are my Father, and You know better than I do what I need. Because you love me, I can pray very simply . . . O God, be not far from me.

—Matthew 19:14; 6:7-9 msg; Psalm 38:21

✨ *Practicing the Spiritual Life* ✨

1. When and/or why are we sometimes tempted to pray with fancy words?

2. When are you most likely to pray a simple prayer?

3. Describe a time you prayed without words and God answered.

4. In what ways can simple prayer keep us open to the Holy Spirit's leading?

CHAPTER 11

WHY PRAY?

We also pray always for you that our God would
count you worthy of this calling,
and fulfill all the good pleasure of His goodness
and the work of faith with power,
that the name of our Lord Jesus Christ may be glorified in you,
and you in Him, according to the grace of our
God and the Lord Jesus Christ.

—*2 Thessalonians 1:11-12* NKJV

"O LORD, you have examined my heart and know everything about me. You know when I sit down or stand up. You know my thoughts even when I'm far away. You see me when I travel and when I rest at home. You know everything I do. You know what I am going to say even before I say it, LORD. You go before me and follow me. You place your hand of blessing on my head. . . . I can never escape from your Spirit! I can never get away from your presence!" (Psalm 139:1-5, 7 NLT).

So, I wonder after reading this passage, *why pray?* God is sovereign and He knows everything about us—our every need, our every desire, and everything that will happen to us from the beginning of our time here on earth to the end of our days. God knows everything we have said and everything we are going to say.

So, then, why pray?

We pray because Jesus loves us and desires to have a personal relationship with us. "This is how God showed his love for us: God sent his only Son into the world so we might live through him. This is the kind of love we are talking about—not that we once upon a time loved God, but that he loved us and sent his Son as a sacrifice to clear away our sins and the damage they've done to our relationship with God" (1 John 4:9-10 MSG).

We pray because the Lord wants us to know Him better and love Him more. Ron and I have been married fifty-five years. Our love for each other has grown over time as we have supported each other through the various seasons of our lives—through hard winters that tested our faith and our marriage; through springtimes of new beginnings that stretched us and grew us; through warm and restful summers that provided relief from trials; and through the learning periods of autumn that challenged us to adapt and change.

In the same way, our love-relationship with the Lord changes over time as we pray and grow in our dependence on Him. As the Lord faithfully sees us through our various seasons of life, we draw closer to Him in greater trust, and our love for Him grows deeper and richer. He draws us to Himself with His loving kindness (Jeremiah 31:3).

Time spent in prayer grows in us the ability to love the Lord with more of our heart, more of our soul, and more of our mind (Matthew 22:37). Two people who love each other desire to be together and to share each other's life, and that kind of precious relationship between the Lord and us grows when we pray.

We pray because we need to confess our wrongdoings and our wrong thinking. Daily, hourly, moment by moment, we sin. Since unconfessed sin blocks our communication with God, we need to pray and confess our sin. It's as simple as that.

We pray because we need the Lord's guidance and direction in everything we do. Our heavenly Father promises to lead us by ways we have not known, along the unfamiliar path of each new day. Surely He will guide us, turn the darkness into light before us, and make the rough places smooth. He will never forsake us (Isaiah 42:16).

We pray because the Lord is our greatest source of help and strength in trying times. Whenever heartache overwhelms us, we become more keenly aware of our need to pray. We recognize our total dependence on God when we have no one else to help us.

The more we share our sorrows with the Lord and seek the reassurance found in His Word, the more we are aware of His caring presence. The Holy Spirit is the Source of all our comfort, the only One who is always beside us, at all times in all our troubles, who is our constant support in suffering (2 Corinthians 1:3-5).

We pray because that is the way to find out how the Lord will provide for our needs and what He wants us to do in the process. We may have no idea how to get what we need, but the Lord knows our needs, and He will guide us toward fulfilling them when we seek His direction.

We pray because we need to be changed by the Lord so that we may glorify Him. God's purpose for us is—above all else—that we love Him, glorify, and honor Him. By our obedience He transforms us into His likeness: "As the Spirit of the Lord works within us, we become more and more like him and reflect his glory even more" (2 Corinthians 3:18 NLT 1996). Through prayer, the Lord transforms us by renewing our minds so that we no longer conform to the world's ways (Romans 12:2).

Our main reason for praying is not to get answers but to know the Lord more personally, to understand and do His will, and to bring Him glory. Then we are able to see His answers more clearly. That's why our prayers need to shift away from being focused on the answers we want; we need to focus on God Himself. If I don't see my most important requests answered, but if I grow in faith, see His transforming work in my life, and become more centered on Him and not on self, then His will is being accomplished in my life.

We pray for ourselves and intercede for others because it is the way we see the Lord at work in our own life as well as in other people's lives. When we pray for and with others, we are not only encouraged by what the Lord is doing in our lives, but we see His work in their lives, which also strengthens our faith. Those we pray for are lifted up and encouraged. One of the highest ways we express our love for others is to pray with them and for them.

We pray Scripture because we often don't know what to pray, but we can present our needs to God in His words. Here is an example of praying Scripture:

"Jesus, You have been teaching me to put off my old self, which is corrupted by deceitful desires, to be made new in the attitude of my mind and to put on a new self, created to be like You in true righteousness and holiness . . . Lord, I ask you to give me a new heart and put a new spirit within me; remove from me a heart of stone and give me a heart of flesh. Fill me with Your Spirit and move me to follow Your decrees and to be careful to keep Your laws . . . For Your eyes range throughout the earth to strengthen those whose hearts are fully committed to You" (from Ephesians 4:22-24; Ezekiel 36:26-27; 2 Chronicles 16:9).

We can praise the Lord using Scripture because we need to express our gratitude and glorify Him. Here are words of praise using Bible verses:

"Lord, with all the earth I make a joyful sound to You. I serve You with gladness! I come into Your presence with singing! I know, Lord, that You are God! It is You who made me, and I am yours. I belong to You; I am a sheep of Your pasture. I enter Your gates with thanksgiving and Your courts with praise! I give thanks to You and bless Your name! For You are good, and Your steadfast love endures forever, and Your faithfulness to all generations . . . Praise You, Lord. Praise You for Your mighty deeds; praise You for Your exceeding greatness!" (Psalm 100; 150:1-2 RSV)

We pray because our prayers are precious to the Lord, as a picture from Revelation clearly illustrates: the living beings and twenty-four elders will fall down before Jesus the Lamb, holding golden "bowls filled with incense—the prayers of God's people!" (Revelation 5:8 NLT1996). Later, incense mixed with the prayers of God's people will be offered on the golden altar before His throne. And the smoke from the incense, together with the prayers of the saints, will go up before God (Revelation 8:3-4). God reminds us that our prayers matter to Him. What a gift that reminder is!

⌁ *Prayer* ⌁

I will lift up my eyes to the hills. Where does my help come from? My help comes from You, Lord, who made heaven and earth. You will not let my foot be moved; You who keep me will not slumber; indeed, You who keep Israel will neither slumber nor sleep. Lord, You are my keeper; You are my shade at my right hand. The sun will not smite me by day nor the moon by night. You will preserve me from all evil; You will preserve my soul. You will preserve my going out and my coming in from this time forth and forevermore . . . You are able to save me completely because I come to You, God, through Jesus, who always lives to intercede for me.

—PSALM 121 KJV AND RSV; HEBREWS 7:25

⌁ *Practicing The Spiritual Life* ⌁

1. Review this chapter's list of reasons to pray. Which one is most meaningful to you? Why do you think that is?

2. Now that you've read this chapter, you are better prepared to answer the question "Since God knows everything anyway, why do you pray?" Write your answer in your own words.

3. Jesus is interceding for you at God's throne (Romans 8:34 and Hebrews 7:25). What does that promise mean to you? How can this promise strengthen your prayer life?

4. Why does having a prayer partner strengthen your prayer life? If you have a prayer partner, list some of the blessings you've experienced. If you don't have a prayer partner, make that an item of prayer!

CHAPTER 12

OPEN YOURSELF TO GOD'S PRESENCE

Draw near to God and
he will draw near to you.

—James 4:8, NKJV

Let's look more closely at what it means to pray as we go about our daily life.

Ironically, the explosion of inventions to make our lives easier has, instead, made our lives more complicated and harder to manage. Social media, countless websites, and hundreds of television channels entice us to give them our devoted attention. Church and volunteer activities also beckon us. Our own schedules and desires often conflict with our sense of duty to others. We may become so overwhelmed by all there is to do that we feel exhausted and deprived of time for ourselves.

Henri Nouwen described the consequences like this: "Our lives are fragmented. There are so many things to do, so many events to worry about, so many people to think of, so many experiences to work through, so many tasks to fulfill, so many demands to respond to, and so many needs to pay attention to. Often it seems that just keeping things together asks for enormous energy . . . This fragmentation is probably one of the most painful experiences of modern men and women."[28]

When our lives are so noisy and so busy, what can we do to develop the discipline of opening ourselves to God and listening to the Spirit's promptings? When so many demands tug at us, what steps can we take to learn to speak with our Lord and hear His voice throughout the day?

Those questions are not easy to answer, but we need to wrestle with this issue if we are going to strengthen our relationship with God.

SEEKING GOD IN THE CENTER OF A CYCLONE

Let's take a look into the life and writings of the man who, even today, teaches us the discipline of practicing the presence of God. Brother Lawrence was a humble man who lived in a Carmelite monastery in Paris in the 1600s. He served in a lowly position at the monastery, but he was known for his spiritual wisdom and the great peace with which he lived his life. After his death in 1691, a collection of his conversations and letters about living in God's peace was published as the book *The Practice of the Presence of God*.

When our world is noisy and chaotic and our busy days are radically different from Brother Lawrence's life in a quiet monastery, can we really practice the presence of God as he did? I think so.

According to Brother Lawrence, practicing God's presence is a twofold discipline. First, *it means carrying on a constant conversation with our Lord and confessing our sins as we go about our daily tasks.*

If we are to remain spiritually strong, we need to develop the habit of constantly communicating with God, always listening to Him and responding to Him.

Second, *practicing God's presence means responding to the Holy Spirit's promptings and guidance in the present moment.*

Have you ever been in the middle of your work when you kept feeling a prompting to call someone? You tried to put it out of your mind, but that sense grew stronger. It reached a point that you couldn't think of anything else.

Feeling a bit irritated, you made the call, and when you did, you learned about a serious need that you could meet. You clearly realized that the Lord had prompted you, and you were blessed by the opportunity to do as God desired and to serve that person.

What Brother Lawrence has to say is easy to understand, but it can be difficult to do, as those of us know who have attempted to practice this discipline. Yet practicing God's presence can also bring a deep joy beyond what the world can offer.

PRACTICING GOD'S PRESENCE

The idea of practicing the presence of God puzzled me for a long time. After all, the Spirit of God is always present with us whether or not we are aware of Him.

But the more I read Brother Lawrence, the more I saw that he had many simple yet profound insights to teach us about how to practice God's presence in a richer way and develop a deep personal friendship with Him.

For example, Brother Lawrence wrote, "The holiest, most common, most necessary practice in the spiritual life is the presence of God, that is to take delight in and become accustomed to His divine company, speaking humbly and talking lovingly with Him at all times, at every moment, without rule or system, and especially in times of temptation, suffering, spiritual aridity, disgust and even of unfaithfulness and sin."[29]

How often my thoughts about God and my prayers turn into agitated internal complaints or angry diatribes! Too often I mentally relive past hurts and difficult experiences. How can I be at peace and seek God's presence if I don't let go of those hurts, relationships, and wrongs from the past? As I've tried to constantly think of the Lord and speak to Him, I've learned more about my own thought life, about how it controls me, and how off-center it can sometimes be.

Brother Lawrence worked for fifteen years in the kitchen, "for which he had a naturally strong aversion." At the end of his life, he worked in the shoe repair shop. He told a spiritual leader "that he was very happy there but that he was ready to leave this position as he had previous ones, glad to do any task, however small, for the love of God. ...That he found the best way of reaching God was by doing ordinary tasks, which he was obliged to perform under obedience, entirely for the love of God and not for the human attitude toward them."[30]

Interestingly, for fifteen years Brother Lawrence worked at a job he disliked intensely and would never have chosen to do, but he learned to do any menial task for the love of God. Similarly, I find my own life taken up with work and problems I would never have chosen for myself. I not only dislike them, but I feel angry that I have to deal with them.

Life's troubles disrupt my plans, putting me in situations and giving me tasks that I'd never choose for myself. But with Brother Lawrence's example in my mind, I now try to pray, "Lord God, may You give me the grace to do all my duties and tasks as a loving gift to others and for Your glory. May Your gracious love shine through all that I do."

Consider this description of Brother Lawrence: "When the occasion arose to practice some virtue he always said to God: 'My God, I cannot do this unless You enable me to do so,' and he was immediately given the strength needed, and even more. That when he had stumbled, he simply acknowledged his fault and said to God: 'I shall never do otherwise if You leave me to myself; it is up to You to keep me from falling and to correct what is wrong.' With this he put the pain of this fault from his mind."[31]

I, too, fall constantly: I forget God as I go about my daily life and often lapse into wrongful thoughts. Brother Lawrence's simple confession reminds me that the Lord desires me to go to Him with childlike trust and confidence and then put the fault from my mind. Rather than clutch guilt, embarrassment, or shame, I need to confess my sins, let them go, and return to my ongoing conversation with my Lord.

Brother Lawrence shared this wisdom as well: "We must continually work hard so that each of our actions is a way of carrying on little conversations with God, not in any carefully prepared way but as it comes from the purity and simplicity of the heart . . . I keep myself in His presence by simple attentiveness and a loving gaze upon God, which I can call the actual presence of God or to put it more clearly, an habitual, silent and secret conversation of the soul with God."[32]

Do you see the significance of Brother Lawrence's point? The secret to more deeply knowing God's presence with us is to carry on a conversation with Him as we go about our day. This kind of conversation means talking to the Lord at all times and in all places, not just during devotions or at church. Every hour—every minute—of our day is an opportunity for communion, adoration, and intercession for others.

Now consider what Brother Lawrence said about how spirit and action work together: "God is a spirit; therefore, He must be worshiped in spirit and in truth; that is to say, by a humble and genuine act of adoration from the very depths of our soul. Only God can see this adoration, which if repeated often will eventually become natural for us as if God were one with our soul and our soul one with God: practice will make us understand this."[33]

When I first read this, I realized that I'd been trying to seek God's company, but more on an intellectual level than in any heartfelt way. I was settling for surface conversation rather than entering into a transparent, genuine, and personal conversation with God. My intellect may be my starting point for practicing God's presence, for singing songs and hymns to Him, for conversing with Him, but then—with the Lord's help and with practice—I can move on to heartfelt devotion.

When I sing the same song over and over or say the same verse or prayer, for example, I fear it is nothing more than vain repetition, a mere babbling of words. May the Lord help me to find balance. Singing the same song to the Lord or repeating the same verse can deliver me from anger, bitterness, depression, fear, spiteful thoughts, and ungodly imaginations when what I say to the Lord and my heartfelt devotion become one. Sometimes it takes action to bring about heart change.

Brother Lawrence also wrote, "We must carry out all of our actions with care and with wisdom, without . . . a distraught mind; it is necessary to work peacefully, tranquilly, and lovingly with God, begging Him to accept our work, and by this continual mindfulness of God we shall crush the head of the devil and cause his weapons to fall from his hands."[34]

These words cause me to ask: *What would God have me do now, today, this week? Am I making the best use of His time?* So often I think of time as my own. I'm always struggling to finish what I should do, the ordinary duties, so that I am free to do what I want to do. I hurry to finish this or that mundane task so I can get to what I enjoy. All of this, of course, leaves God out. In practicing His presence, I've become more aware of how I use His time, of what He would have me do instead of what I want to do.

God longs for our prayers to turn to adoration of Him, to our recognition of His great love for us. Brother Lawrence put it this way: "During our work and other activities, during our spiritual reading and writing, even more so during our formal devotions and spoken prayers we should stop as often as we can, for a moment, to adore God from the bottom of our hearts, to savor Him . . . These interior retreats to God gradually free us by destroying [our] self-love."[35]

And I long to increase my moments of adoring God! Yet how quickly my prayers turn to concerns about myself. Brother Lawrence must have had similar struggles, because he added this encouragement:

"All these acts of adoration should be made by faith, knowing that God is truly in our hearts, that we must adore, love and serve Him in spirit and in truth, that He sees everything that happens and will happen to us and to all His creatures, that He is independent of everything and all creatures depend on Him."[36]

Offering the Almighty God our constant adoration doesn't change the reality of our trials. But praising God and giving Him thanks for the blessings of life will lift us above our concerns and shift our focus from our own needs to joy in His presence.

⌒

We cannot remain constantly in God's presence by our own volition or in our own strength. But we can more easily practice the presence of God when we remind ourselves that God is drawing us to Himself and that His Holy Spirit dwells within us. Furthermore, God seeks us even when we don't seek Him. So we don't have to bear the burden of seeking God. Jesus is standing at our heart's door, knocking and beckoning us to come to Him.

Welcome Him into your heart.

Sit in His presence.

Listen and respond. "Lord, here am I."

⌒ *Prayer* ⌒

Can I hide in secret places so that You cannot see me, God? No, I cannot hide from You, for You fill heaven and earth . . . This day I acknowledge and take to heart the truth that You, Lord, are in heaven above and on the earth below. There is no other God . . . And My ways are in full view of You, Lord, and You examine all my paths

...You see my ways and count my every step ... As for me, it is good to be near You, Lord. I have made You my refuge ... You are my Shepherd who gathers me in Your arms, carries me close to Your heart, and gently leads me ... Your eyes are on me because I fear You; my hope is in Your unfailing love ... Keep me as the apple of Your eye; hide me in the shadow of Your wings.

—Jeremiah 23:24; Deuteronomy 4:39; Proverbs 5:21;
Job 31:4; Psalm 73:28; Isaiah 40:11; Psalm 33:18; 17:8

⟋ *Practicing the Spiritual Life* ⟍

1. Describe a time you clearly sensed God's presence with you. Why do you think it happened then and there?

2. Brother Lawrence particularly disliked working in the kitchen, but he had to do it every day for years. What task do you have a "strong aversion" to but you have to keep doing it? What can you do to practice God's presence as you do that particular task?

3. Do you feel that God is far away from you because of a particular concern or difficulty? If so, write a note asking Him for assurance of His unfailing presence with you.

4. What does it mean to you that God wants to be with you? What impact does that truth have on your practice of His presence?

5. In what ways do we practice God's presence through praise?

CHAPTER 13

HOW TO PRAY SCRIPTURE

Pray in the Spirit on all occasions
with all kinds of prayers and requests.
With this in mind, be alert and
always keep on praying for all the saints.

—*Ephesians 6:18*

Several years ago a friend wrote me a letter expressing her fears about hardships she and her family were suddenly dealing with. Her husband had lost his job due to a change in company ownership, and he couldn't support his family on the minimum-wage jobs in the rural area where they lived. He finally found a job several hundred miles away, so the family uprooted their teenagers, leaving one high schooler behind. In addition, several family members had serious health problems.

In her letter, my friend shared the fears she felt in their new situation: "I think the thing I'm having the hardest struggle with is trying to get victory over my fear. I'm scared because we have no money in the bank, no life insurance for my husband, and no health insurance for the rest of us. I'm scared about his health and mine and about his job. I'm scared for our son on his own and our other kids who want to return to our hometown. Scared because I can't find a job, and juggling bills every month is becoming more difficult. What if something happens to our house? What if one of our ancient cars croaks? I have my devotions and feel strengthened, but then the phone rings and my heart drops, and I think: What next?"

After I read my friend's letter and prayed for her family, I felt as if my intercession for them was less than adequate. I, too, often wondered for myself, *What next?* As for my friend's situation, I wondered what difference my prayers would make since the family's difficulties seemed so enormous.

My friend and her family had to move once more, but God provided both her and her husband with jobs and medical coverage. Even so, they wouldn't have chosen to make those moves or go through such hardships.

When we pray for the seemingly impossible, our sense of helplessness often seems greater than our faith. We're not alone. David, Elijah, Job, Jeremiah, Naomi, Paul, and many others in the Bible felt alone, forsaken, and helpless.

Their prayers ranged from simple requests asked in childlike faith to the cries of the brokenhearted seeking to understand an incomprehensible tragedy. Some prayers were quiet intercession offered alone in a room; other prayers were anguished pleas for safety by those feeling abandoned in the deserts and mountains. Scripture is also filled with joyous exclamations of celebration, praise, and worship.

According to Scripture, we can share every need with our Lord— our unspeakable sorrows and even those things we consider too trivial for His interest. Prayers offered by God's people in Scripture show us many ways we may come before Him, no matter how we feel.

PRAYING SCRIPTURE

Even though God had answered many of my prayers in wonderful ways, I sometimes used to feel that my intercession for others was ineffective. When I lacked the words to intercede for others, I often prayed a psalm. But it wasn't until I read Sarah Gudschinsky's article "Lord, Bless Charles" that I discovered the principle of praying passages from God's Word, whatever the need.

Gudschinsky remembered the turning point in her prayer life. She was praying for fellow Wycliffe missionaries on the day designated for them in the organization's prayer directory. Suddenly she realized that she didn't know many of them personally, and she didn't have any recent news about them.

She wrote this: "My prayer is dry and hurried and impersonal—bless the Grubers, and bless . . . Wait a minute! The next name on the list is my own. And I wonder with shock and horror if others today are praying: 'And bless Sarah and bless Shirley . . . and . . .' —not really praying for me at all . . . It occurs to me if I use Scripture as a base for my prayer, it may become more meaningful—more like the [kind of] prayer I need from others."

So Gudschinsky started personalizing Scripture for each person she prayed for. She chose Colossians 1:9-13 to pray for a missionary named Charles. Verses 11–12 read, "Strengthened with all power according to his glorious might so that you may have great endurance and patience, and joyfully giving thanks to the Father." She personalized this and prayed: "Strengthen Charles with all Thy glorious power—the power that raised Christ from the dead. Take his weakness and inability, that it might be lost in the ocean depths of Thine own omnipotence. Teach him patience and long-suffering. Make him patient with the shortcomings and irritating habits of his co-workers. Enable him to extend grace despite the daily annoyances and friction. Make him patient despite interruptions. Give him long-suffering when unreasonable upsets arise and delays slow the work. And grant to him patience with himself, with his own faults and weaknesses."

That article had opened me up to a whole new dimension of praying God's Word. Since then I've written many personalized Scripture prayers. I find that when I pray Scripture, I am praying more in line with how God would have me pray for myself and others.

SCRIPTURE PRAYER CARDS AND NOTEBOOKS

If you struggle to know how to pray and what words to use, you may find it helpful to write Scripture prayers on index cards, on the computer, or in a blank book. Here are some suggestions:

- Write your requests with paraphrased Scripture so you can address God intimately with His words.
- Personalize a verse or passage with specific references to a given situation.
- Write prayers and praises using a phrase, verse, passage, or several verses from different chapters in the Bible that either speak to you or address the needs you're concerned about.

- If you have more requests than you can cover during a single devotional time, intercede for certain people on Monday, other ones on Tuesday, and so on throughout the week.

- Read the passage in several different versions of the Bible and then write a prayer that includes words from many, if not all, of those versions.

- Find an appropriate verse and insert the names of the people you are praying for. As you pray John 3:16, for instance, include the names of people and pray for their salvation.

- Personalize a prayer using more than one passage. This example uses Colossians 4:12, Proverbs 4:26-27, and Ephesians 6:10. (I've used the name *Jim* as an example): "Lord, I'm constantly wrestling in prayer for Jim that he may stand firm in all the will of God, mature and fully assured ... Make level paths for his feet, and may he take only the ways that are firm. May he not swerve to the right or the left; keep his feet from evil. May Jim become strong in You, Lord, and firm in Your mighty power."

WAITING IN EXPECTATION

When we search for appropriate Scripture passages, we will discover how to pray for a specific person or need. The verses will also help us intercede according to God's Word.

As we seek guidance, the Holy Spirit may speak to our hearts and impress upon us where we can obtain help for the person's situation.

The Lord sometimes uses us to answer our prayers or to lead us to the person who has the exact information needed to solve a problem.

But often our concerns far outweigh our ability to resolve them. That's then the wisest course is to record our requests, continue to intercede using Scripture prayers, and wait upon our Sovereign Lord to answer.

Many of us have felt discouraged because we've waited years without our heartfelt prayers being answered. It took me a long time to realize that the source of my discouragement was not my lack of faith but my expectations about how I presumed God should answer.

We often have definite expectations of when and in what manner God should answer our prayers. Our faith may be genuine, and God is hearing our prayers, but we need to realize that the people we're praying for have the freedom to do and think as they please.

Though the Holy Spirit is speaking to the people we're interceding for about their spiritual needs, they're free to say to God and us: "No." "Not now, maybe later." "I don't believe in God." Or "I have my own religious beliefs." Others may have committed a crime or be in bondage to addictive sins they're unable or unwilling to be freed from, and they don't think God could possibly accept or forgive them.

People who once expressed faith in the Lord may simply lose interest or be bitter toward God because of a disappointment or a hurtful experience with another Christian or the church. Our hope and encouragement comes from having the confidence that God hears our prayers, and He is working behind the scenes in the lives of those we're praying for. Jesus and the Holy Spirit are also praying with us according to God's will for those we're concerned about.

Of course our expectations may not be met nor our prayers answered in the way we desire. But the purpose of prayer is not to gain the answers we want. The purpose is to persevere without ceasing, to never give up, and to believe that God desires to hear from us and desires to answer. When we pray, we receive the Lord's strength, are reminded of His support, and are blessed by His tender care. We remind ourselves of His great faithfulness and remember that we can trust Him no matter how He chooses to respond to our prayers.

Writing out Scripture prayers is a good way to gain the strength we need to pray with perseverance. If you choose to keep a record of your prayers, be sure to go back and note the date when your prayers were answered. Also include a few thoughts about how God guided or intervened, blessed or protected. Remember to write brief prayers of rejoicing and thanksgiving next to the requests that you've seen God answer—and remember that God answers yes, no, or "wait."

Speaking of answers, I encourage you to write answers to prayer in a separate notebook. Every few months go back and read this testimony to God's great faithfulness. You'll be blessed and encouraged by these reminders of the ways God has led you and those you love safely through trials you had long forgotten about. You'll be strengthened by this first-hand account of God's never-failing presence in your life—and you'll soon be adding more praises!

⌇ *Prayer* ⌇

Our Father in heaven, hallowed be Your name . . . Blessed be Your glorious name, and may it be exalted above all blessing and praise . . . Your kingdom come, Your will be done on earth as it is in heaven . . . Teach me to do Your will, for You are my God . . . Give me this day my daily bread . . . Teach me, Lord, to treasure the words

*of Your mouth more than my daily bread . . . I will forgive others their trespasses,
and then You will also forgive my trespasses. And lead me not into temptation, but
deliver me from evil . . . For no temptation has seized me except what is common to
others. You are faithful, God; You will not let me be tempted beyond what I am able
to bear. But when I am tempted, You will provide a way out so that I can stand up
under it . . . For Yours is the kingdom, and the power, and the glory, forever. Amen.*

—Matthew 6:9 kjv; Nehemiah 9:5 amp; Matthew 6:10 kjv;
Psalm 143:10 kjv; Matthew 6:11; Job 23:12; Matthew 6:12-
13; 1 Corinthians 10:13; Matthew 6:13 kjv

ᷡ *Practicing the Spiritual Life* ᷡ

1. Have you, like Sarah Gudschinsky, prayed "dry and hurried and impersonal" prayers? When? Why?

2. Why can praying Scripture lead to a more intimate relationship with God?

3. You've been praying Scriptures at the end of each chapter of this book. Comment on this experience.

4. Some of our most urgent requests remain unanswered despite our persistence in prayer. Are you about to give up praying for certain concerns, desires, or people—or have you already stopped completely? Either way, ask the Lord to show you how to intercede according to His will. Then write your own prayer that includes His Word and your requests.

Part Four

THE

TESTED

LIFE

CHAPTER 14

BEING CRUCIFIED WITH CHRIST

*May I never boast except
in the cross of our Lord Jesus Christ,
through which the world
has been crucified to me,
and I to the world.*

—*Galatians 6:14,* NIV

After my husband, Ron, retired, we moved to the central coast of California, and he went to work again as an auto parts salesman. Every weekday he drove past miles of vineyards, rows of strawberries, open land dotted with cattle and oak trees, and rugged terrain that overlooked the Pacific Ocean.

He loved his job and the chance to drive through the breathtaking countryside. Then, fourteen years ago, he was an hour's drive north of us in Atascadero when he suddenly had a stroke in his left eye and went blind. It was as if the connection between his eye and his brain had been cut like an electrical wire, but could not be spliced together again. Many years before that, he had lost the sight in his right eye, also due to a stroke.

He pulled over to the right but kept driving—blind. God, in His mercy, guided Ron safely all the way home, and my husband never drove again. Our lives were turned upside down. This man whom I had always depended on now had to depend on me. Thus began a nightmarish journey. Both Ron and I have had cancer. I went from being hard of hearing to being deaf. We both have diabetes, and I have sleep apnea, restless leg syndrome, and a balance center disorder.

This was not the fun, easy retirement life I had envisioned, but God was taking me on a journey that would reveal to me His sovereignty and teach me what it means to live the cross-bearing life.

Though our health struggles were difficult, worse testing came that nearly crushed us all—yet God not only drew me closer to Him than I had ever imagined possible, but I also saw Him work in amazing ways.

A LONG STRUGGLE

Our son and his wife could not have biological children, so they applied to our county's foster-adopt program. Six months later, while they were finishing the classes required to be foster parents, they received a call to pick up a baby girl from a hospital in another town.

When we went to the hospital to pick up baby Grace, the social worker told us that the goal was to return the baby to her mother. This surprised me, and although I never forgot those words, I tried to dismiss that option as impossible.

I took care of Grace while our son and his wife worked. Grace had such an endearing personality that we all fell in love with her. Six months later, however, the social worker's words proved true: Grace was returned to her mother. Our hearts broke beyond description. Grace's mother did not have a job, a car, or clothing for the baby. She was living in a halfway house for a time, but when she was kicked out, she and Grace were on the streets.

We decided that since we couldn't have Grace, we would "adopt" her mother and help her along. I grew to love Grace's mother, and I prayed for her constantly. She had been raised in an abusive family and hadn't finished seventh grade. Our church helped furnish an apartment for her, and she found a job at a nearby convalescent home.

The mother let us take care of Grace when she was working and often on weekends, but she continued to make poor choices. She gave birth to two more daughters by different addicts and felons over the next four years, and all of the girls were neglected, often hungry, and even left alone for hours.

In spite of reports to the child protection agency by the mother's neighbors and other people as well, social workers did not intervene or require the mother to follow through on food programs and parenting classes. One of her daughters had a severe speech handicap, but her mother would not get the help her daughter needed.

Finally, after being endangered for years, the girls were removed from their mother when one of her drug tests was positive. All three girls were turned over to my son and his wife. I took care of the girls during the day. Though my husband is blind, he is amazingly self-sufficient, so he helped with household chores and caring for the girls. Still, I had the majority of the responsibilities.

After our family had the girls for about two years, their social worker informed us that she was going to return the girls to their mother who was now living in a tiny room in a homeless shelter. The mother and three daughters would be sleeping in a bunk bed. During the day she would be out on the streets with the girls.

After such a long ordeal to keep the girls safe, our family was devastated to hear they would be returned to their mother. If that happened, we would not be allowed to see them. We pleaded with the authorities, but we were losing hope. *Where was God? How could He not intervene?* We were heartsick.

I cried out to God again and again, but I rarely had devotions. I was in church. I prayed with many other people, but I questioned and doubted and raged at God.

Finally, thanks to court-appointed volunteers who monitored the mother and reported to the court, our son and his wife were able to adopt the two older girls. Their younger sister was adopted by a family perfectly suited to care for her special needs.

What I share here barely begins to tell the story of all that happened during that intense season in our lives. The adoption was final when Grace was six and a half. Today, the girls still struggle emotionally, and we continually pray for healing.

Questions still haunt me: *Why didn't God intervene sooner? Why would He allow those girls to be hurt when we were praying so hard and an army of friends stood with us interceding? Why did God not change the hearts of those social workers who believed that children belong with their mother no matter how badly they are abused?*

I don't have answers. In fact, the struggles in our family are not much better today than they were fourteen years ago. So what is God teaching me? He is teaching me that my walk with Him is not about me or about the answers to prayer I so desperately want. It is all about Him and His plans for my family and for me. It is all about leading the cross-bearing life.

LESSONS FROM THE CRUCIFIED LIFE

One thing I have learned is that our faith can be so tested that we blame God for the loss and the pain and, consequently, don't spend time with Him when we need Him the most.

If that sounds like your struggle, I pray you will open yourself to God and to seeing Him work in and through your life despite the darkness of the hour. Expecting God to answer in ways you dictate to Him, however, is not faith. It is presumption. God is Sovereign, and He does as He pleases. If you have had a period of time away from the Lord, as I did, He is waiting to welcome you home.

Once you release your expectations to God, you will find yourself freed to watch Him work in you and around you. Open your heart to God when nothing changes or when situations become even worse. Listen carefully for His voice, stay alert for evidence of His presence, and you will begin to see Him and your life in new ways—and what you see Him do will increase your faith. Let me share an example.

As I shared in the introduction, many years ago when I first began writing about the devotional life, I felt as if I was solely responsible for my spirituality.

I thought that if *I* read my Bible and followed certain spiritual disciplines, *I* would become a woman of God. *I, I, I!* It was all up to me! But God used that difficult time of waiting for the girls to be pro-tected to remind me that *He* is the Sovereign God whom I must trust even when circumstances don't make any sense and terrible things are happening.

During those years, I constantly struggled with my attitude and my desire to somehow flee the pain. God took me to the foot of the cross, where I begged, complained, and pleaded for His intervention and mercy. I wanted Him to take the hurt away.

Then God began to show me the cross-bearing life that Jesus taught: "If any of you wants to be my follower, you must turn from your selfish ways, take up your cross, and follow me. If you try to hang on to your life, you will lose it. But if you give up your life for my sake, you will save it. And what do you benefit if you gain the whole world but lose your own soul? Is anything worth more than your soul?" (Matthew 16:24-26 NLT). Let's look at each part of this passage in light of God's sovereignty and the cross-bearing life.

Jesus says, "Be my follower." Did I have a sincere and genuine desire to follow Christ? I thought so—until my faith was tested to the extreme. Then I had a choice to make: live the retired life that I wanted or do what God had called me to do, which was intervene on behalf of the girls and take care of them.

During those years, I felt powerless, abandoned, and devastated spiritually. Everything I'd ever believed about prayer and about God had crumbled. I struggled with debilitating depression and could barely function, but I had to keep moving forward. Now since the adoption and with those difficult years behind us, I see the great joy that our grandgirls bring to us.

Jesus invites us to follow Him—but the invitation comes with certain conditions. Those conditions are costly. That's why we find ourselves tempted to turn away from God: the life we are striving to have and the things we want are of greater importance to us than Jesus. We don't want to give them up to follow Jesus.

But I can assure you that when we do let them go—or when they are taken from us as part of God's plan—we find greater peace and spiritual fulfillment than we ever would have known if we had sought after things rather than follow Jesus.

Jesus calls us to "turn from your selfish ways." You and I are free to do as we please. We can go after what our heart desires, gain the things we want, and profess to be Christians. Then we can cling to those treasures while ignoring the promptings of God, who calls us to sacrifice what we want for His sake.

When the girls were infants and toddlers, I complained to God that I was too old to help raise young children. God reminded me of Sarah in the Old Testament who gave birth when she was one hundred years old. God was calling me to sacrifice my dreams for the greater dream of a better life for our adopted granddaughters.

In my hardest moments, though, I feared my faith would be utterly destroyed. But God in His mercy began to teach me about His sovereignty. He put me in difficult situations that He knew I could not walk away from. He entrusted me with the most heartbreaking experiences of my life because He knew I would fight with all my being for what was right.

In the process, I changed. I began to turn from my selfish desires; I began to submit to God's desires for me. It was and continues to be a hard journey. But because I know Jesus's promises, I see that the pain of this life will one day fade away in the light of heaven's glory.

Jesus calls us to "take up your cross, and follow me." When we submit to the life God has chosen for us rather than clinging to the life we want, we are obeying Jesus's call to be crucified with Him. We may be put in places we never would have chosen for ourselves, we may find ourselves doing things we would never have imagined doing, and we may experience losses that break our hearts. Yet surrendering our plans and desires to the Lord is what Jesus calls His followers to do.

Today I can't imagine our lives without our granddaughters. They bring us great joy, and I am so thankful we chose to follow Jesus because the blessings have far outweighed the heartbreak.

Jesus told us to not "try to hang on to your life, [or] you will lose it." Recently I went to an estate sale. The house was enormous, and the rooms and hallways overflowed with china, dolls, hats, holiday decorations, jewelry, knickknacks, sewing machines, and more. All these things the deceased woman had collected and cherished were now being picked over by strangers. I wondered how she would feel if she could see what was happening to her precious treasures.

We can waste our life accumulating things. We get an emotional high as we anticipate buying something, but once we own it, we are left feeling empty, so we find ourselves craving some other thing. Our treasures and the false life they represent can so consume us that we lose our life collecting things rather than surrendering to Christ, deny-ing ourselves, and following Him.

This truth applies not only to physical possessions. Striving for earthly affirmation, position, security, or simply the life we want also keeps us from loving God above all else. We hold tightly to treasures we will one day lose instead of living for a joy that no one can take from us.

Jesus said, "If you give up your life for my sake, you will save it. What do you benefit if you gain the whole world but lose your own soul? Is anything worth more than your soul?"

Dietrich Bonhoeffer wrote this: "Everything which keeps you from loving God above all things, everything which gets between you and your obedience to Jesus, is the treasure to which your heart clings."[37]

Our earthly life is brief. My life has passed so quickly. It's hard for me to fully grasp that I am in my latter years—and I have wasted so much time on unimportant things, on things that are worth nothing compared to spending all eternity in heaven with Christ. Interestingly, it is the pain in my life that helps me see most clearly what is worth focusing on, what is worth sacrificing for.

My soul is of great eternal value, and so is yours. We were created by God and for God: we were created to bring Him glory! So now is the time to give up the life we want. Now is the time to follow Jesus. Now is the time to hang on to our life in God and forever gain our soul.

THE GOD-DISCIPLINED LIFE

Now consider another one of Jesus's teachings: "Unless a kernel of wheat falls to the ground and dies, it remains only a single seed. But if it dies, it produces many seeds. The man who loves his life will lose it, while the man who hates his life in this world will keep it for eternal life" (John 12:24-25).

Just as a kernel of wheat must die before it can grow into mature stalks of grain, so must we human beings die to our old self before we can be mature believers.

Moreover, when wheat is harvested, it's threshed to separate the seed from the straw. Some seeds are saved to be replanted; other seeds are crushed and ground into flour.

The wheat harvesting process is a picture of our personal and spiritual lives. The Holy Spirit nurtures seeds of spiritual trust in our minds and hearts, cultivating the fertile soil until sprouts of faith grow into mature stalks. Then He threshes and sifts our lives to separate seeds of faith from the straw of mistrust.

The wheat-growing cycle illustrates aspects of the discipline process that God uses in our lives to develop in us stronger faith and greater spiritual maturity. Submitting to this process means surrendering to God's discipline, and His discipline brings us to the point of either dying to self or turning away from Him and rebelling.

Enduring this often-hard sifting process is essential to one's spiritual maturity. But we have no desire to "endure hardship as discipline" (Hebrews 12:7). We long for an easy, peaceful, simple life free of trials. We desire the blessings of the Christian life, but not the burdens. We long for freedom to live as we please, the freedom to be what we want to be, the freedom to have it our way, the freedom to have our many desires met.

Yet—as author and theologian Elton Trueblood pointed out—"we have not advanced very far in our spiritual lives if we have not encountered the basic paradox of freedom, to the effect that we are most free when we are bound . . . The one who would like to be an athlete, but who is unwilling to discipline his [or her] body by regular exercise and by abstinence, is not free to excel on the field or the track . . . With one concerted voice the giants of the devotional life apply the same principle to the whole of life with the dictum: Discipline is the price of freedom."[38]

God is teaching me that essential to a disciplined life is obedience and that the God-disciplined life is the way to true freedom. At the heart of genuine obedience is reverential fear, humble submission to, and unconditional love for our Lord—even in the midst of life's most devastating circumstances and our deepest heartaches.

DYING TO SELF, LIVING TO GOD

During those years of fighting for my grandchildren, my faith was tested so severely that all I could pray was *God, hold onto me. I don't want to lose my faith.* With every painful setback, I wanted to turn away from God. But where would that lead me? I knew that without God, I would have nothing. Left to follow my own ways, I fail every time.

So even though the thought of making spiritual goals seemed senseless, even though reading the Bible was nearly impossible, I prayed. I begged others to intercede, and they did. I asked God to hold on to me when I couldn't hold on to Him. And He did.

God was teaching me that His plans and ways were not mine. That I would never understand this side of heaven why Ron went blind and the girls were abused. God's ways are mysterious, but out of the worst trials He can bring solid ministry and glory to His name.

Have I recovered spiritually from these horrible trials? No, I haven't. I still struggle with questions and with a sadness that strikes me unexpectedly. But I also rest in a deep, God-given peace that makes no sense in light of what has happened.

And God continues to teach me how to watch for His work in my life even when circumstances are not what I would choose. So I am continuing to learn to live each day on His terms, to obey His instructions, to live in the moment, and to not dwell on how desperate my problems may seem. Simply put, I am learning what it means to be crucified with Christ.

↝ *Prayer* ↜

Lord, You are my shepherd. Even when I "walk through the valley of the shadow of death, I will fear no evil, for you are with me; your rod and your staff, they comfort me" . . . I may make plans for my life, but You direct my steps . . . So by Your grace may I turn from my selfish ways, take up my cross, and follow You. If I try to hang on to my life, I will lose it. But if I give up my life for Your sake, I will save it. After all, what do I benefit if I gain the whole world but lose my soul?

—Psalm 23:4; Proverbs 16:9 nkjv; Matthew 16:24–26 nlt

↝ *Practicing the Spiritual Life* ↜

1. When has God used circumstances in your life to remind you that He is sovereign?

2. What in your life situation, if anything, keeps you from spending time with God? Why?

3. What difficult life circumstances—if any—seem as if they'll never change? In what ways is God using that pain to facilitate your dying to self and your experiencing being crucified with Christ?

4. What comfort might God want to give you?

CHAPTER 15

RECOGNIZING LIFE'S UNCERTAINTIES

"For I know the plans I have for you," declares the LORD,
"plans to prosper you and not to harm you,
plans to give you hope and a future.
Then you will call upon me and come
and pray to me, and I will listen to you.
You will seek me and find me
when you seek me with all your heart."

—Jeremiah 29:11-13

Blinding sunlight streamed into my car window early on that June evening. I felt tense as I tried to focus on the road ahead with its mass of moving vehicles. I was traveling from Orange County to Santa Maria, more than a three-hour drive from southern California to mid-state.

It had been a quick two-day trip jammed with appointments and visits with family. I was tired and on the verge of getting sick, although I didn't realize it at the time. All I could think about was getting home.

I decided to drive straight through without stopping. It was seven o'clock, and I figured the after-work traffic would quiet down from a roaring growl to a tame snarl. But when I reached Long Beach, traffic was deadlocked. I was going to be inching my way up the freeway if I didn't take a detour.

I was near a freeway that would take me into central Los Angeles and through the most dangerous part of that city, but at least traffic was moving on that road. I prayed for safety and took this alternate route. I was greatly relieved when I passed out of the dangerous area and into more familiar territory.

It wasn't long before I approached the turnoff where I usually take a fast-food break and work out some of the knots that came with sitting behind the steering wheel. I ignored the gentle nudging to stop. As I drove on and passed familiar rest areas, I kept ignoring the Holy Spirit's quiet prompting to take a break.

By the time I was about forty minutes from home, it was dark. I was weary, dreaming of my own bed and a good night's rest. But when I came around the next bend, a bright red neon sign blinked at me: "Detour! Detour! Detour!"

Highway 101 was closed. (I later learned that a large section of the road had slid into a sinkhole at a construction site.) Within seconds, I found myself on the two-lane winding, treacherous, and totally unfamiliar Highway 1.

I found myself squeezed between two huge trucks and unable to see around the one in front of me. I kept a wary eye on my rearview mirror as the double-trailer gravel truck behind me kept pressing in too close. Suddenly, the gravel truck roared into the oncoming lane. The empty truck bounced, rattled, and rumbled as it thundered past both my car and the truck in front of me. In that heart-stopping moment I was sure we'd have a horrendous accident.

The night was so black I couldn't see anything on either side of the highway. The only assurance I had was an occasional fluorescent orange detour sign with an arrow pointing the direction I was moving.

When I reached a junction, I saw a patrol car sitting by the road. We were being routed to another highway. For a second I thought about asking the patrolman for directions to a road that would take me directly to Santa Maria. I knew it was close by, but I had no idea how to find it. The truck was still in front of me, however, and instead of stopping, I kept following like a sheep that has no idea where it is being led.

I hadn't been on the second highway long before I realized we were doubling back in the direction we had come. If only I had stopped to ask for help, I would have been home in twenty minutes; now I had a fifty-minute drive ahead of me.

And by now I was more than exhausted and in desperate need of a rest break. Finally, I reached the town of Buellton. I was grateful to see lights, but all the places where I could stop were closed. I quickly found the Highway 101 off-ramp and eventually made it home safely.

After that trip, I thought about the "if onlys." *If only* I'd listened to my husband and waited to drive home the next morning. *If only* I'd listened to the quiet nudging of the Holy Spirit to take a break. He knew about the detours, and He knew I needed some rest and relief. And perhaps avoiding the stress would have saved me from the bladder infection that afflicted me afterward.

Wondering about the "if onlys" can't change what happened that night, but I did gain some important insights from that experience. I realized, for instance, that we encounter similar detours in life, detours that send us on a roundabout way to our destination. The uncertainties we feel during those major life detours try our faith and test our willingness to follow God. If we hope to remain faithful to the Lord, we need to be mentally and spiritually prepared for those unsettling and unscheduled detours of life.

LIFE'S DETOURS

Life's detours are sometimes just brief inconveniences, but other times they take us along dark, long, and terrible roads. In fact, we may never return to the main highway again. The death of a loved one, divorce, a terminal illness, the loss of a job—the list of major life detours is endless.

Yet if we're going to lead a holy life, we need to be spiritually prepared for detours. It's those unexpected deviations from our expectations and plans, from the ways we thought God would work in our life, that plunge us into the dark night of the soul and cause us to question our faith. Life may seem leaden black. We may feel lost and alone as we travel an unfamiliar road with its hairpin curves and heart-stopping dangers.

But consider this: detours are not just irritating interruptions that prevent us from easily reaching our destination. They are actually a well-planned part of our spiritual journey. God often desires to guide us in a way we would never choose for ourselves. We want to drive on the easy road that takes us straight home. But God may send us on a circuitous route because He has a divine appointment or essential spiritual lessons for us and for others. The Lord uses even our darkest detours to encourage others who find themselves lost on a similar road as well as to deepen our relationship with Him.

When I started writing this book, I came down with a severe infection. With my energy depleted from being sick, I could hardly concentrate as I tried to write. I made little progress. My emotions hit a new low as I also struggled with depression. How could I do what I thought God wanted me to do? It seemed as if He was working against His own plans for my life. Certainly, He was sifting me in the very areas I was writing about. I felt spiritually chastised and challenged.

But I'm learning and relearning that the pressure, stress, and sorrow related to unexpected detours are meant to draw us closer to the Lord. He is able to redeem for His own glory the most disappointing heartaches and terrible trials. Do we see those trials as an embittering experience, or do we consider them an opportunity for the Lord to graciously reveal Himself in a new and unforeseen way? Until our faith is refined and strengthened by a detour on a dark road, we will only see God as the means of satisfying our own needs and serving our own purposes.

LIFE'S CHANGES

Sixteen years ago my husband and I moved from Garden Grove, California, to Santa Maria. I had been hired to teach English as a Second Language classes at the local community college. Ron retired from the company he'd worked at for almost twenty-three years and planned to look for something else in our new hometown.

When we moved, I was excited but uncertain about teaching new vocational classes at the college. I had not done that before, and my previous job was far more secure. I knew that a teacher's schedule would vary from semester to semester because student enrollment was highly unpredictable. If not enough students enrolled, the class was closed, and I didn't earn a paycheck.

Ron thought he had work before we first moved to Santa Maria, but all of his options fell through while we were moving. We were apprehensive, but he found a position the first week he was here.

Then he lost that job due to a change in company ownership. We wondered if we would be able to stay in Santa Maria, where jobs are scarce and salaries are low. After a month he found work, but then that company announced it was selling the business.

Shortly afterward, we lost our medical insurance. We soon discovered that individual medical premiums were unaffordable. My fear level went off the charts.

The following morning, as I started to read the day's selection in the *One Year Bible,* I felt prompted to read the psalm from the day before. This was the message God had for me: "I am still confident of this: I will see the goodness of the LORD in the land of the living. Wait for the LORD; be strong and take heart and wait for the LORD" (Psalm 27:13-14).

The next day as I was eating breakfast, I drew a card from our box of promise verses. It was the same passage from Psalm 27. God's gracious reassurance gave me the peace to accept the uncertainties we faced.

In Proverbs we read, "Do not boast about tomorrow, for you do not know what a day may bring forth" (27:1). Paul wrote, "Now, compelled by the Spirit, I am going to Jerusalem, not knowing what will happen to me there" (Acts 20:22).

Life's uncertainties can definitely challenge my confidence in God. I know in my mind that God is faithful and reliable, but I waver emotionally. I would rather not go through the wrenching process of my faith being tried and stretched. I'd like to be a spiritual superperson, but I'm not. And I suspect I'm not alone. Yet as I persevere by faith, my trust in the Lord grows stronger.

If we expect to have a secure, stable life without heartaches, then we will be disappointed in the Lord. Our faith will be in our expectations and not in God Himself. Faith is certainty in God—not in the answers we desire or the outcome we have decided we want.

If we're going to become women with a heart for God, we need to realize that life can be painfully uncertain. We may have a very clear idea about how God should change the uncertainties we're facing. God, however, desires to transform our faith from shallow belief and self-centered preoccupation into an abiding, unshakable confidence in Him. As He does that work in our heart and our life, the certainty of our faith becomes real.[39]

After all, life constantly changes, whether we stay in one place or move every year. God "changes times and seasons; he sets up kings and deposes them" (Daniel 2:21). One of our greatest temptations is to stop walking with the Lord when our circumstances or relationships get difficult.

When change comes into our lives, we need to ask: "Lord, what are You trying to say to me through this experience? What do You desire to teach me? How do You want to use this in my life to glorify You and to minister to others?"

Will we allow the Holy Spirit to make Christ real in us no matter how trying the changes that come? Will He so manifest His presence in our lives that others clearly see Jesus in us?

What happens to us is not for our sake alone, but for the sake of Christ and others. Certainly, God is refining us, so what happens is for our sake too. But the Lord always wants to take us beyond ourselves. He has far more to accomplish: He longs to reveal Himself through our greatest heartaches as we demonstrate to others our reliance on Him.

LIFE'S UNKNOWNS

In his epistle, James had this warning for us: "Now listen, you who say, 'Today or tomorrow we will go to this or that city, spend a year there, carry on business and make money.' Why, you do not even know what will happen tomorrow" (4:13-14).

The author of Ecclesiastes wrote, "A man cannot discover anything about his future" (7:14). And Jesus said, "Do not worry about tomorrow, for tomorrow will worry about itself. Each day has enough trouble of its own" (Matthew 6:34).

Looking back over my life, I would never have predicted what has happened to Ron and me—neither the good nor the bad. Because I have a strong need for security, I sometimes feel anxious and even fearful about the future. But I remember the joy that God has brought out of difficult situations in the past. I remember how He is shaping me to desire Him most of all.

God wants us to have peace about an uncertain tomorrow, and He wants us to trust Him regardless of our changing circumstances. This is the challenge and the joy of living the tested life.

ᓚ *Prayer* ᓗ

Lord, I do not know the future, and no person can tell me what is to come. I do not have power over the wind to contain it; so I do not have power over the day of my death . . . Yet You will lead me when I cannot see, by ways I have not known, and along unfamiliar paths You will guide me. You will turn the darkness into light before me and make the rough places smooth . . . I am uncertain about what will happen, but You, Lord, go before me and will be with me; You will never leave me nor forsake me. Therefore, I will not be afraid; I will not be discouraged. I will be strong and courageous. . . . I will trust in You at all times; I will pour out my heart to You, for You are my refuge.

—ECCLESIASTES 8:7–8; ISAIAH 42:16; DEUTERONOMY 31:8, 6; PSALM 62:8

ᓚ *Practicing the Spiritual Life* ᓗ

1. If you are on an unexpected detour right now, how are you feeling? What truths in this chapter were especially encouraging? What would it look like to seek God's direction as you travel those detours?

2. When has a change in your life brought about something good that you did not anticipate? Give a specific example or two.

3. Why is trusting God about an uncertain future a joy as well as a challenge?

4. What does it mean to *actively* wait on God?

CHAPTER 16

PRESSING ON
IN PAINFUL
CIRCUMSTANCES

Praise be to the God and Father of
our Lord Jesus Christ, the Father of
compassion and the God of all comfort,
who comforts us in all our troubles,
so that we can comfort those in any
trouble with the comfort we
ourselves have received from God.

—*2 Corinthians 1:3-4*

It can be easy to fall into Santa Claus Christianity: all we have to do is present to God our long wish list, and He'll give us what we ask for.

The truth is, God promises suffering as well as blessings. We read in 1 Peter, "Dear friends, do not be surprised at the painful trial you are suffering, as though something strange were happening to you" (4:12). Proverbs 14:13 says, "Even in laughter the heart may ache, and joy may end in grief." Joys and sorrows always come mixed together, and it's the sorrows more than the blessings that strengthen our faith if we allow them to. When the trial is over, we are better able to see the Lord's guiding hand helping us through those difficult times. Yet, we would never want to go through them again.

When disaster whipped into my life like a raging firestorm and burned everything to ashes, I surveyed the charred rubble surrounding my family and felt spiritually incapacitated. I saw no resolution close at hand, and I knew that my life would never be the same as it was before. Yet I found new life through the lengthy labor of suffering.

As the following learned-from-real-life proverbs state, our life may be filled with heartaches:

Life can be difficult and painful, especially when events seem utterly senseless.

Life presents us with challenges and disappointments we'd never choose to deal with.

Life poses problems we cannot humanly solve.

Life can be as unpredictable as a devastating earthquake.

Life can be unfair, and justice may not be done here on earth.

Life may bring terrible diseases to our body and brain and painful conditions that modern medicine cannot heal or even relieve.

Life may confront us with trials that cause us to question our faith.

Those proverbs may sound pessimistic, but anyone who has suffered knows how true they are. When bright hopes burn to ashes, when tragedy that makes no sense in human terms crashes in on us, the authenticity of our faith is challenged as never before.

Our spiritual life is either deepened or weakened during those tough times. Only if we choose to trust in God's sovereignty and His deep love for us will our faith survive life's trials.

THE TRUTH ABOUT TOUGH TIMES

A sure way to collapse spiritually is to believe that we know best what God should do for us and for those we love when the trying times come. It's natural to want the pain to end, but we may turn away from the Lord when we focus on trying to find answers rather than focusing on Him.

For example, when we realized after many eye surgeries and laser treatments that my husband's eyesight could not be restored, I questioned God's presence. Then when the outcome of our fight for our foster granddaughters was contrary to everything I prayed God would do, I asked, *How could God not intervene and change the heart of the social worker?*

We need to accept three hard facts about tough times if we're going to get past our pain and glorify Christ in the midst of it.

First, we are not exempt from suffering. We do not have special privileges. Everyone in the world experiences difficulties.

Second, we don't always gain relief from pain. The trials we experience may not be resolved and may actually grow worse. Some afflictions and diseases may last for many years and others for a lifetime.

I see this in the lives of several of our Christian friends whose children are alcoholics or drug addicts or have committed crimes and spent time in jail. Their children continue to self-destruct despite the fact that their parents have seen them through rehabilitation programs, sought hours of Christian counseling, prayed faithfully, and done all that they know to do. Our friends remain faithful to their Lord, but the enormity of their unrelenting trials is heartbreaking.

Third, a crisis of faith often occurs when suffering strikes. One of the greatest threats to maintaining our commitment to Christ is the painful trials of life. That decisive moment comes when we must choose either to continue to trust our Lord or to turn away from our faith in Him. That moment can come suddenly, or it can recur over a prolonged period that's been filled with adversities. This crisis can be triggered by something as minor as a simple misunderstanding or as major as the painful death of someone we love.

WORKING OUT OUR FAITH IN STAGES

Just as we go through grief-crisis stages when we experience a severe trial or the death of a loved one, we go through faith-crisis stages. When our faith grows stronger at times, then weaker, and then takes a different shape, we are better prepared to work through our grief as our Holy Comforter reaches out to us with His healing grace.

The way we find relief from our sorrow and overcome a crisis of faith is by doing the work of grieving. We may not move through this process as quickly as we desire, and if our trials are ongoing, we may move in and out of the stages of grief and faith-questioning for years.

Though we may work through those stages and reconcile ourselves to the outcome, some heartaches remain with us for a lifetime. They are particularly intense on an anniversary, birthday, holiday, or other moment meaningful only to us. As we open ourselves to Christ's healing love, however, those times of sorrow diminish.

Here are some principles that helped me grow spiritually stronger as I worked through the grief that came with my crisis of faith:

Christ's act of reconciliation on the cross redeems our sorrows. Our Savior not only died for our sins, but He died for our pain. Consider that "suffering makes sense only when we join it to the saving work of Jesus. Apart from Jesus, it is a problem without a solution."[40]

Christ identifies with our pain and shares our griefs. "He was despised and rejected by men, a man of sorrows, and familiar with suffering . . . Surely he took up our infirmities and carried our sorrows" (Isaiah 53:3-4).

Jesus desires to see His Father glorified through our afflictions just as He glorified His Father when He died on the cross. Moreover, Christ arose from the grave to bring us out of death into newness of life. That is the hope He has given us, and by faith we believe that, like Him, we will be resurrected from this painful world.

All suffering is spiritually significant for Christians. As we went through trials, I sought after answers from God Himself. Why did He allow this heartache? How could God possibly care about us when He let us go through such a senseless tragedy? Wrestling with questions like these helped me, and I finally came to the conclusion that we human beings will never obtain a satisfying earthly reason for why we experienced such trials. The why behind our suffering is a mystery that will only be answered in heaven—but it will be answered.

We find spiritual meaning by comforting others with the same comfort we received from the Lord during our own trials (2 Corinthians 1:3-7). We care for those who are hurting even when we still need healing ourselves. The Lord redeems our sorrows by using us to touch the hearts and lives of others with His tender, caring mercy.

Isaiah said, "The Lord GOD has given me the tongue of those who are taught, that I may know how to sustain with a word him that is weary" (50:4 RSV). Our caring Counselor will give us the wisdom and words we need to comfort those who are hurting. Often these dear folks simply need us to listen with an empathetic heart. The Lord may even lead us to start or join a special care ministry. Some of the finest ministries were born out of the founder's devastating losses and pain.

Trials will strengthen our trust in Christ if we work through our grief and our crisis of faith. During the painful stages of grief, we may experience anger and depression, despair and overwhelming sorrow. We may feel numb and in shock, abandoned and isolated. We may ask why. We may try to bargain with God about our trials, promising Him that we'll change or do certain things if He'll quickly solve the problem or bring healing.

As we work through our grief, we may eventually come to the final step of accepting the outcome and reconciling ourselves to the difficult changes in our lives.[41]

CRISIS OF FAITH

Throughout the grief stages, we may feel so shattered that we don't see how we can trust the Lord. We may feel spiritually broken and bereft of our faith, totally unable to trust God for a period of time.

The Old and the New Testaments are filled with the heart-rending cries of hurting saints. Yet patriarchs, prophets, disciples, and godly women who had crises of faith still clung to their God, sought His help, and expressed their trust in Him. We, too, can find renewed faith when we cry out to God. The psalms in particular are filled with heartfelt expressions of grief that we can offer to the Lord when we are hurting.

Even in our brokenness, a tiny seed of confidence in God will grow deeper spiritual roots. We can cling to our Lord no matter how terrible the heartaches, despite our inability to handle the painful circumstances, and regardless of our doubts about God and our wavering faith. We can ask God to hold on to us when we can't hold on to Him any longer, and He will.

As we work through a crisis of faith, we may come to accept trials as a part of life. We may come to the place of trusting the Lord to see us through any kind of suffering. We may keep relying on Him even when serious problems remain unresolved. Yet the thought of experiencing further heartache is often more than we can bear. In His grace, God enables us to endure any unexpected trials that strike.

Above all, our Redeemer will heal and forgive us when we confess our lack of trust in Him. He will empower us to overcome our defeated faith. Our holy Comforter will tenderly love us and care for us. Our mighty God will uphold us and give us the courage we need to endure affliction.

And we will safely pass through our crisis of faith and find ourselves spiritually renewed as we are reconciled both to our Savior and to the outcome of our difficulties. For "if anyone is in Christ, he is a new creation; the old has gone, the new has come! All this is from God, who reconciled us to himself through Christ and gave us the ministry of reconciliation ... We are therefore Christ's ambassadors, as though God were making his appeal through us. We implore you on Christ's behalf: Be reconciled to God" (2 Corinthians 5:17-18, 20).

BEAUTY FROM ASHES

Suffering challenges us to change. Although we may not be able to resolve the circumstances that bring our greatest heartaches, we can change our angry, bitter, and unforgiving attitude, our way of handling grief, and our relationship to the Lord.

We may try to escape our troubles by denying them, but the pain only becomes worse as we continue to run away from them. Denial keeps us from seeking godly guidance and working through our grief. We can only *change our response to trials* by recognizing their reality and by doing the work of grieving, by facing the painful circumstances, and by seeking the help and support we need.

We can also *change our attitude and feelings about our trials.* If we remain angry and unforgiving, we become hard, unkind, and bitter people. Then we not only hurt ourselves, but our bitterness hurts others.

Some people cling to their grief and never move beyond their tragic experiences. Because they feel God has abandoned them, they no longer grow in their faith and commitment to Him. They become self-absorbed and obsessed by their pain.

If we face the pain that comes with the toughest of trials, if we work through our grief, and if we let ourselves receive the Lord's healing comfort, we are freed to grow in our spiritual life. We are freed to become caring people able to extend grace, kindness, and love to those around us.

Finally, we can allow suffering to *change our relationship with the Lord.* As we are reconciled to Him in all our afflictions, as we place ourselves in His presence and do what we can—despite our pain—to maintain an intimate friendship with Him, His Spirit will sustain us.

Remember that usually the only thing about our heartaches we can change is our attitude toward them, and that attitude is closely related to our choice to have faith in God. We will experience tragedies and losses that will remain a mystery this side of heaven. Trusting God in those mysteries brings Him the greatest glory.

Once we do the work of grieving and we release our sorrows to our ever-caring Comforter, we will experience a God-given peace that is far stronger than our pain. As we lay our broken lives before God, He will change us so we become more like Jesus, a compassionate servant of the poor and brokenhearted.

Paul knew pain and Paul knew transformation: "Though outwardly we are wasting away, yet inwardly we are being renewed day by day" (2 Corinthians 4:16). Our faith is refined and purified as we glorify Christ in all our afflictions, no matter how trying they may be (1 Peter 1:6-7). Finally, as we persevere by faith, we become "mature and complete, not lacking anything" (James 1:4).

✐ *Prayer* ✐

"O my Comforter in sorrow, my heart is faint within me" . . . "You have taken my companions and loved ones from me; the darkness is my closest friend" . . . "I have no refuge; no one cares for my life" . . . Yet in Your great mercy do not put an end to me or abandon me, for You are a gracious and merciful God. Now therefore, great, mighty, and awesome God, You who keep Your covenant of love, do not let all this hardship—this hardship that has come upon me—seem trifling in Your eyes. . . . Turn my mourning into gladness; give me comfort and joy instead of sorrow.

—Jeremiah 8:18; Psalm 88:18; 142:4; Nehemiah 9:31-32; Jeremiah 31:13

✐ *Practicing the Spiritual Life* ✐

1. Describe a time when you found spiritual meaning in suffering. Be specific about the circumstances as well as the lesson you learned.

2. What do you need to guard against in times of suffering? When you're enduring difficult times, what changes do you need to make in your attitude and your life so that you can remain strong in your faith?

3. What are some of your natural attitudes and reactions to unkind treatment and suffering? In what areas of your life do you especially need the Lord's grace so you can respond to injustice in a godly way?

4. Write a prayer affirming your trust in God despite the pain and heartaches in your life. Remember, you don't need to *feel* trust in God to do this. Praying, writing, and acting out trust will help build your trust.

CHAPTER 17

RELINQUISHING YOUR HEART'S DESIRES

During the days of Jesus' life on earth,
he offered up prayers and petitions
with loud cries and tears to the one
who could save him from death,
and he was heard because
of his reverent submission.

—*Hebrews 5:7*

"Hold my hand," said Katelyn.

My two-year-old granddaughter, her brother, Byron, and I were at the pond in the park. Katelyn loved to feed the ducks and geese, but their honking, quacking, and squabbling scared her. She felt safe as long as she could hold my hand and stay beside me while she watched them gobble up puffy white kernels of popcorn.

Another time we had an electrical blackout when I was watching Katelyn for a few hours. By evening it was black both outside and inside the house. She didn't seem to be afraid of the darkness. She played with a flashlight, turning it off and on and shining it in her face. We even read an animal picture book by flashlight.

I put her to bed at eight-thirty and lay on the bed beside her. She didn't say a word, but she reached out to find my hand.

She tossed and turned trying to fall asleep—and she never let go of my hand. Every time I released her hand to see if she had fallen asleep, she reached out in the dark until she found mine. When I thought she had finally fallen asleep, I got up.

I dressed for bed and then heard her call me in her small quiet voice, "Grandma?"

"Would you like apple juice or milk?" I asked.

"Juicy," she answered.

I got her a bottle of juice and lay down beside her again. She drank her bottle with one hand and held mine with her other hand until she finally fell asleep.

AN UNSEEN HAND

Just as Katelyn needed the security of holding my hand, we need the sense of God's unseen hand holding ours. We need that comfort when we experience frightening trials . . .

About fifteen years ago, before Ron lost his sight, he went through a sudden medical crisis. I panicked when, just as we received the bad news from Ron's doctor, we learned about the impending loss of medical insurance and the possibility that Ron would lose his job as well.

At the same time, our son was working as a night custodian at an elementary school in a gang-infested area. He had to make almost nightly police calls because of drug dealings and gang activities. Despite repeated requests for protective fencing and gates, they were never installed.

I felt nearly paralyzed with concern for my husband and my son. I remember one morning opening *My Utmost for His Highest* by Oswald Chambers. I randomly turned to a devotional titled "The Never-Failing God."

There Chambers referred to Hebrews 13:5-6: "For he hath said, I will never leave thee, nor forsake thee. So that we may boldly say, The Lord is my helper, and I will not fear what man shall do unto me" (KJV). Then he wrote this: "Have I really let God say to me that He will never fail me? If I have listened to this say-so of God's, then let me listen again."[42]

Here I was: I definitely needed to listen again and again. Then I read the next day's devotional: "God says—'I will never leave thee,' then I can with good courage say—'The Lord is my helper, I will not fear'—I will not be haunted by apprehension. This does not mean that I will not be tempted to fear, but I will remember God's say-so. . . . Faith in many a one falters when the apprehensions come; they forget the meaning of God's say-so, forget to take a deep breath spiritually. The only way to get the dread taken out of us is to listen to God's say-so."[43]

Reading these words, I realized that I was filled with apprehension, dread, and panic—and that I did not have the slightest confidence in God. As I pondered those devotionals and prayed, I began to release my fears to the Lord. I took His unseen hand, and peace returned.

About a month later Ron's health stabilized, and we learned that he was going to keep his job after all. But I treasured the peace I had known even before the circumstances changed.

THE PRAYER OF RELINQUISHMENT

Many years ago I read Catherine Marshall's book *Beyond Our Selves.* Her chapter "The Prayer of Relinquishment" had a profound effect on my spiritual growth, strengthened my relationship with the Lord, and helped me maintain my faith.

Marshall wrote this: "If relinquishment is real, the one praying must be willing to receive or not receive his heart's desire."[44] When Satan weakens our confidence in the Lord, it almost always involves our heart's greatest desires. We are most vulnerable to spiritual defeat and wavering trust when our earthly longings go unmet. Through the prayer of relinquishment, though, we become focused on God's will and His desires for us. We open ourselves to seeing how God will answer our prayers in His own way.

But relinquishment is more than words we pray; it is an act of surrender. We give over to God the control of our desires. We stop holding onto them emotionally, mentally, physically, and spiritually. We even renounce them. We refuse to allow ourselves obsessive thoughts about what we need. We seek pastoral or professional help if we find ourselves unable to stop these thoughts.

Someone we love or an important possession is difficult enough to relinquish by choice. When the relinquishment was not our choice—when it was prompted by circumstances we could not control—the process can be even more painful.

Our desires may not be sinful; they may be holy. We may be praying for people to find salvation or to recommit their lives to the Lord. And we all have legitimate needs. Nonetheless, we have to relinquish to the Lord all these requests and desires as well as our ambitions, our health, our material goods, our imperfect life, our personal rights, and—most of all—the people we love. Again, although our desires may be for good things, our ultimate desire needs to be for God and His will for us.

Relinquishment, however, is not resignation, and it doesn't mean that we stop praying. As Marshall wrote, "Resignation is barren of faith in the love of God. It says, 'Grievous circumstances have come to me. There is no escaping them . . . So I'll just resign myself to what apparently is the will of God; I'll even try to make a virtue out of patient submission.' So resignation lies down quietly in the dust of a universe from which God seems to have fled, and the door of Hope swings shut."[45]

Relinquishment doesn't weaken our hope; instead, it strengthens our confidence in the Lord. False hope believes that God will meet our needs according to our specifications. Genuine hope is in God Himself, not in how He might answer our prayers.

Marshall summarized it like this: "Faith is by no means absent in the Prayer of Relinquishment. In fact this prayer is faith in action . . . And the act of placing what we cherish most in His hands is to Him the sweet music of the essence of faith."[46]

HINDRANCES TO FAITH

What hindrances to our faith result when we're unable to relinquish our desires to the Lord? There are many. We become more focused on ourselves. We presume upon God to answer our prayers in a narrow, prescribed way. We dictate to God exactly what He should do. Then when He doesn't answer as we determined or He takes too long, we're disappointed.

Another option we have is to deny reality and pretend that we don't have any heartaches or unmet desires. We may give the impression that all is well when behind this spiritual facade, our lives are actually falling to pieces. We may convince ourselves either that God is going to do a miracle or that He will quickly grant us the answers we hope for.

Consider what author Larry Crabb said: "That hope [that God will give us what we want], however, is a lie, an appealing but grotesque perversion of the good news of Christ. It's a lie responsible for leading hundreds of thousands of seeking people into either a powerless lifestyle of denial and fabricated joy or turning away from Christianity in disillusionment and disgust. It's a lie that blocks the path to the deep transformation of character that is available now."[47]

We want our pain to be over now, but it is those very trials that test and refine our trust in the Lord. When our lives are shattered, our faith can be purified. Hard times show us how willing we are to lead a holy life and how genuine our faith in God is.

During these hard times, we need to be transparent before the Lord about our heartaches. We need to allow ourselves to grieve. We may need to deal with anger, anxiety, or depression. We may bitterly accuse God of failing us as the heavens remain silent in response to our prayers and nothing changes. It's essential to realize that this is part of working through our grief—but if we lock ourselves into those darker places, we will not be able to complete the relinquishment process.

Do we desire to be holy, or do we desire to be blessed? Is our motive for following God rooted in the answers we expect to receive from Him? Is our commitment to Christ based on having good feelings, good times, and good health?[48]

As long as we want God to serve our own purposes, He is not Lord of our life. But when we relinquish our desires and needs to Him, we are prepared for Him to do whatever He pleases. Until we take that step of relinquishment, we'll be bound by our fears as we anxiously wait for the answers we want from Him.

As Marshall pointed out, "We know that fear blocks prayer. Fear is a barrier erected between us and God, so that his power cannot get through to us. So—how does one get rid of fear?"[49]

Before answering that question, Marshall acknowledged that letting go of fear "is not easy when the life of someone dear hangs in the balance, or when what we want most in all the world seems to be slipping away. At such times every emotion, every passion, is tied up in the dread that what we fear most is about to come upon us. Obviously only strong measures can deal with such a powerful fear."[50]

We could humble ourselves at any point along the way, but we prideful human beings don't do that. Instead, it's when we feel we have no emotional, physical, or spiritual reserves left that we humble ourselves before the Lord and admit the power of our fears and weakness, just as the psalmist did. Who more than David poured out his fright before the Lord? "Fear and trembling have beset me; horror has overwhelmed me" (Psalm 55:5).

THE PROCESS OF RELINQUISHMENT

I've found that I need to work through the process of relinquishment in order to release my concerns and be relieved of my all-consuming fears. Praying with a partner and relying on the Word of God help me the most. I also write out both my concerns and the Scriptures that speak to my fears.

I choose to cling to the promises of God, promises such as "I am the LORD, your God, who takes hold of your right hand and says to you, Do not fear; I will help you" (Isaiah 41:13).

Sometimes I open my hands and hold them out to the Lord, or I lie facedown on the floor with my hands stretched out as an act of relinquishment.

I may repeat a paraphrased Scripture prayer like this one: "I will not fear, for You are with me: I will not be dismayed, for You are my God. You will strengthen me; yes, You will help me; yes, You will uphold me with the right hand of Your righteousness" (Isaiah 41:10 KJV).

Acceptance is another key aspect of relinquishment. As Marshall put it, "Acceptance says, 'I trust the good will, the love of my God. I'll open my arms and my understanding to what He has allowed to come to me. Since I know that He means to make all things work together for good, I consent to this present situation with hope for what the future will bring.' Thus acceptance leaves the door of Hope wide open to God's creative plan."[51]

The final step in relinquishment comes when the Lord's plans for us become our heartfelt desires: "Delight yourself in the LORD, and he will give you the desires of your heart. Commit your way to the LORD; trust in him, and he will act" (Psalm 37:4–5 ESV).

How often we focus on just one part of this passage: "He will give you the desires of your heart." We put all our hopes in our own desires and think only of how desperately we want God to grant them. But we have skipped over the first part of the verse and the conditions vital to having the desires of our heart granted.

Psalm 37:4 calls us to delight in the Lord, to express our gratitude to Him for who He is and what He means to us apart from what we desire and what He gives us. Furthermore, as we commit our way to the Lord, we let go of *our* desires so that His desires may become ours. Then, as we trust completely in Him, He will grant us the desires of our heart, because now our desires and His are the same.

⌒ *Prayer* ⌒

"How long must I struggle with anguish in my soul, with sorrow in my heart every day?" . . . "My grief is beyond healing; my heart is broken." . . . "Have mercy on me, LORD, for I am in distress. Tears blur my eyes. My body and soul are withering away" . . . "My heart is filled with bitter sorrow and unending grief" . . . But You, O God, see my trouble and grief; You consider it to take it in hand. I commit myself to You, for You are my helper. . . . Show the wonder of Your great love to me, You who save me by Your right hand, for I take refuge in You from my foes. . . . You hear my desires when I am afflicted; You encourage me and listen to my cry . . . Now Lord, I relinquish those I love into your hands. Search us, O God, and know our hearts; try us, and know our anxious thoughts. See if there be any wicked way in us, and lead us in the way everlasting.

—PSALM 13:2 NLT; JEREMIAH 8:18 NLT; PSALM 31:9 NLT; ROMANS
9:2 NLT; PSALM 10:14; 17:7; 10:17; 139:23-24

⌒ *Practicing the Spiritual Life* ⌒

1. If you're sorrowful and troubled about a need that God wants you to relinquish to Him, express your feelings to Him.

2. Do you struggle to relinquish to the Lord your desires, ambitions, health, material goods, imperfect life, personal rights, and—most of all—the people you love? If so, explain.

3. Whom, if anyone, do you need to forgive as you work through

the process of relinquishment? Write out a prayer asking God to guide you and help you through this process.

4. Do you feel as if your willingness to relinquish your life and your desires to God is being tested? Why? What might God give you in place of what you give up?

CHAPTER 18

RELEASING
YOUR LIFE TO GOD

I thank Christ Jesus our Lord, who has given me strength,
that he considered me faithful, appointing me to his service.

—*1 Timothy 1:12*

During World War II as the Nazis tried to take over Europe, Corrie ten Boom and her family hid Jews and members of the Dutch resistance in their home. After an informant reported on the family's activities, the ten Booms were arrested and incarcerated in a prison in Holland. In her cell Corrie often prayed, "Lord, never let the enemy put me in a German concentration camp."[52]

But when Corrie was in her fifties and her sister, Betsie, was fifty-nine, they were shipped in a railroad boxcar to the Ravensbrück concentration camp in Germany where more than 96,000 women would die. There they experienced atrocities of evil almost beyond description.

In that torturous camp, Corrie and Betsie held clandestine Bible studies twice a day. Many women who had never heard of Jesus came to know Him as their Savior. Corrie said, "If God had not used my sister Betsie and me to bring them to Him, they would never have heard of Him. Many died with the name of Jesus on their lips. They were well worth all our suffering."[53]

Betsie died at Ravensbrück. The week after her death, Corrie was standing with the ranks of women prisoners during roll call. When her number and name were called, Corrie wondered what it meant. The prisoners were never called by name.

As she stood in the freezing weather in her ragged prison dress, she wondered if she would soon join her sister in heaven. She thought it would be her last chance to witness for Christ, so she began sharing the gospel with Tiny, the girl standing next to her who had never read the Bible.

Other prisoners nearby listened as Corrie told them how her sister had just died and that Jesus was always with them no matter how much they had suffered. He had freed Corrie from hating her enemies even though she had lost so many members of her family to the death camps.

As they stood for nearly three hours, Corrie continued telling Tiny about Jesus, and the girl accepted the Lord. That very morning Tiny died, but by a divine "clerical mistake" Corrie was released from Ravensbrück. The week after her release, all women prisoners her age were murdered.

RELEASING OUR LIVES
TO THE LORD

Corrie experienced the depth of what it meant to release her life in service to the Lord. She had lost in the very bowels of hell all she held dear—her family, friends, freedom, comfort, safety, and security. She had experienced starvation, torture, and the deepest suffering of her life.

After the war, Corrie wanted to return to her town, to the home where she had lived in for fifty-three years and her profession as a watchmaker. But she surrendered her life to God and instead be-came—as she described herself—"a tramp for the Lord."

During the later years of life when many retire, Corrie shared the gospel and her testimony in more than sixty countries. She spoke to thousands of people in many different situations, from the darkest prisons to the grandest churches.

She traveled around the world twice and slept in more than a thousand beds; some were comfortable, and others were straw mats on dirt floors. She lived and ministered as Jesus did: without a place she could call her own. She gave up the security of having a home and the peace of sleeping in her own bed and lived dependent on the hospital-ity of strangers for food, lodging, and financial support.

At seventy-three years of age, she was so exhausted and ill that she wanted to give up her extensive speaking schedule. She decided she would stop traveling and make a home in Africa, but then an African Christian told her about how her words had ministered to him in prison. He read her a passage from Revelation: "Repent and live as you lived at first. Otherwise, if your heart remains unchanged, I shall come to you and remove your lampstand from its place" (Revelation 2:5 Phillips).

She felt convicted. "I had lost my first love," she realized. "Twenty years before I had come out of a concentration camp—starved, weak—but in my heart there was a burning love: a love for the Lord who had carried me through so faithfully—a love for the people around me—a burning desire to tell them that Jesus is a reality, that He lives, that He is Victor. . . . I wanted everyone to know that no matter how deep we fall, the Everlasting Arms are always under us to carry us out."[54]

Corrie asked the Lord for forgiveness, surrendered her "cold heart," and returned to her calling as His tramp. She continued her journeys until she was eighty-five years old. On February 28, 1944, Corrie had gone to prison. Exactly thirty-three years later, on February 28, 1977, she moved into her own home. Though she stopped traveling, she kept up her worldwide ministry.[55]

GOD TEACHES US HIS WAY

You would think that, compared to the cruelty and loss of the concentration camp, life outside prison might have been easier for Corrie. But as she traveled around the world, she continued to suffer hardships and learn many more lessons about releasing her life to the Lord.

She writes, "When I left the German concentration camp, I said, 'I'll go anywhere God sends me, but I hope never to Germany.' Now I understand that was a statement of disobedience. F. B. Meyer said, 'God does not fill with His Holy Spirit those who believe in the fullness of the Spirit, or those who desire Him, but those who obey Him.'"[56]

Corrie did return to Germany, the land of her enemies. With the help of friends, she rented a concentration camp and turned it into a home for refugees. They removed the barbed wire: "Flowers, light-colored paint, and God's love in the hearts of the people changed a cruel camp into a refuge where people would find the way back to life again."[57] During her travels Corrie raised money to rebuild the shelter, and many groups and churches assisted in the work.

Psalm 32:8 had been the life verse of Corrie's parents: "I will instruct thee and teach thee in the way which thou shalt go: I will guide thee with mine eye" (KJV). Corrie wrote, "Now that Father and Mother were gone, this promise became the special directive for my life as well—God's pledge to guide me in all my journeys."[58]

Most of us will not be called to serve God in the extraordinary way Corrie was, but even in our "ordinary" lives, God calls us to yield ourselves to Him so we may serve Him. The Lord has many divine appointments for us to share the gospel and to minister to family, friends, and strangers.

To be women after God's heart, then, we need to release our lives to the Lord so that He may guide and instruct us in the way He desires us to go. As we release our lives to God, He will use us in ways we cannot imagine. He will allow us to go through many experiences that are not meant for us alone. Everything that happens to us is not just about us; it's about what God desires to do through us.

For example, God used a woman named Norma in my life in a special way. I rarely went to church as a child, but when I was sixteen, Norma invited me to her church. One evening she shared with me how to become a Christian. It was the first time I remember hearing the gospel. Shortly afterward I accepted Christ when I was alone in my bedroom.

After being out of touch with Norma for many years, one day I received a call from her. She was surprised when I told her that it was through her witness that I had become a Christian.

When we release ourselves to the Lord, He will use us in ways we may not realize. God used Norma to lead me to the Lord, and that decision changed my entire life.

THE BEST REMAINS

When Corrie ten Boom was in her eighties, she talked to a group of students in the Midwest: "I told them of the joy of having Jesus with me, whatever happened, and how I knew from experience that the light of Jesus is stronger than the greatest darkness. I told them of the darkness of my prison experiences . . . I wanted these students to know that even though I was there where every day 600 people either died or were killed, when Jesus is with you, the worst can happen and the best remains."[59]

Our idea of the best remaining is far different from God's. Why was Corrie spared while her family members were killed? Betsie and their father were in a far better place in heaven, but why did they die such cruel deaths? It's a mystery, and only God knows the answer. The best that remained, however, was Corrie's willingness to serve the Lord even though she suffered such terrible losses.

Releasing ourselves to the Lord does not mean we will be exempt from horrific trials and unfair tribulations. In fact, to draw closer to the Lover of our soul, we need to realize that we may suffer as we serve Him.

The worst can happen, but out of the ashes the best can remain. If we are willing to relinquish our heart and our life, Christ will redeem our tragic losses and release us from the prison of painful experiences.

Even if we have brought on the worst in our life due to our foolish mistakes, rebelliousness, and sins, the Lord will do His transforming work in our lives if we repent and allow Him to, and the best can remain.

CHANGE OF HEART

I have certainly not experienced the kind of suffering and loss that Corrie ten Boom did, yet I have learned similar lessons in my own life. I have given up many things that were good and right, things that I dearly loved, because God had other plans for me.

For instance, I was the director of a preschool and planned to make that my career. Through many different experiences, but mostly by the strong hand of God, I left that field to begin a writing ministry. But I wrote with a rebellious attitude. I'd never wanted to write, and I soon discovered that it was extremely difficult work.

I paid dearly for that attitude, and so did my family. For five years, I suffered from numerous infections. I was on antibiotics for an entire year, I went through two major surgeries, and I experienced many other heartaches and difficulties. Although I wrote and although God kept confirming His will in many amazing ways, I continued to fight against this calling. I published articles and books, but I had not surrendered my will or released my life to the Lord to do with me whatever He pleased.

Gradually—and despite myself and totally by God's grace—I began to have a change of heart. A desire to write about the spiritual life grew in me, yet I felt some kind of inner conflict, and I had no real sense of direction. I felt utterly inadequate and began doubting that I could write anything publishable. My attitude was self-defeating, like the fearful children of Israel who didn't trust the Lord to guide them safely into the Promised Land.

In fact, the greatest fear of my life was that God would become so angry with me that He'd sentence me to wandering in a desert. I feared that my life would be wasted because of my complaining, my lack of trust, and my rebellious attitude. Finally, I reached the point where I didn't feel I could write anything at all.

About that time, God impressed upon my heart that I should return to college and earn a degree. I didn't want to do that either, but I went to school and, strangely, had an urgency to finish. After graduation, I felt led to teach English as a Second Language part-time.

Then I was hired as a book editor for a Christian publisher, and my desire to have a writing ministry returned. During that time, I met with a woman to seek spiritual counsel. When I told her about my personal conflicts over writing, she asked me, "What if you never write again?"

I felt as if my heart had been pierced. *Give up writing? No, I could not accept that.* I left our meeting shaken and more determined than ever to write. But I questioned whether God would use me after my rebellion.

Although at one time my whole being had rejected what God desired me to do, now I had a passion to write. But I was only able to squeeze in a few moments of writing here and there because of my long work hours.

Then the publishing company announced they were moving out of state, and God impressed upon my heart that I should not make the move. I immediately found an excellent part-time teaching position at the college where I had taught before. I needed to work and was grateful for the provision, but I doubted that I'd ever have a writing ministry. Finally, I surrendered my will to the Lord and released my life to Him to do with as He desired.

Although I had rebelled in my heart and had not fully followed the Lord's will for my life, He mercifully redeemed my mistakes. As I look back over those long desert years, I see that God was preparing me for ministry and teaching me many spiritual lessons. I realized that He had been gradually changing my heart attitude. God allowed me to have many different kinds of experiences, both positive and painful, that transformed my faith and my life. I learned that in our journey toward becoming a woman with a heart for God, we may often fail, but God restores us as we renew our commitment to do His will.

As it turned out, about sixteen years passed between the publication of my second book and my third. During those years, God was refining my life and my writing. I kept a spiritual journal, and it became the basis for a devotional Bible study. I am deeply thankful that God redeemed my life and that even when the worst happened, the best remained.

OUR HIGHEST CALLING

Love should be our highest motivation for releasing our life to God. Jesus put it this way: "Whoever has my commands and obeys them, he is the one who loves me" (John 14:21) and "A new command I give you: Love one another. As I have loved you, so you must love one another" (John 13:34).

Being a loving servant is especially a challenge when we minister to difficult people. Corrie ten Boom experienced the highest test of love, the call to love her enemy. At a church in Berlin, her former prison guard came forward and asked her for forgiveness. As he stood before her, she recalled the terrible suffering of her dying sister and felt deeply bitter. Yet in that moment Corrie knew that her inability to forgive the guard was more harmful than his whip.

So she cried, "Lord, thank You for Romans 5:5: 'The love of God is shed abroad in our hearts by the Holy Ghost which is in us.' Thank You, Lord, that Your love in me can do that which I cannot do.

"At that moment a great stream of love poured out of me, and I said, 'Brother, give me your hand. I forgive all . . . ' I could not do it. I was not able. Jesus in me was able to do it. You see, you never touch so much the ocean of God's love as when you love your enemies."[60]

When we release our lives to God, He can work through us in ways we cannot work ourselves. That is the beautiful fruit of living a life devoted to Him.

SURRENDER

God doesn't force us to surrender to Him. He may allow adversity to convict us of our need to submit to Him, but even during these trials, He does not force His way upon us.

Our spirit may be broken. Our health, destroyed. Our emotions, frayed. We may lose loved ones, and every earthly possession may be stripped from us. We may find ourselves at the absolute bottom, yet even then we are still free to say no to God. Even if we feel utterly without hope, we may refuse to submit to God. We may turn away from Him and continue to resist the powerful conviction of the Holy Spirit.

It remains our responsibility to release our life to God so that He may accomplish His will and purposes. God may use circumstances or people to narrow our choices, but we are still free to rebel.

If we are to draw closer to the Lover of our soul, we alone must choose to obey God and submit to His will. When we do, the Holy Spirit will instruct us and teach us in the way we should go (Psalm 32:8). Then, by His grace, God will give us what we need to accomplish all that He desires us to accomplish.

Hear the wisdom of Oswald Chambers: "The tiniest detail in which I obey has all the omnipotent power of the grace of God behind it. If I do my duty, not for duty's sake, but because I believe God is engineering my circumstances, then at the very point of my obedience the whole superb grace of God is mine."[61]

Releasing our life to God in the darkest circumstances is one of the joys of the tested life—a step of faith in the truth that even in pain, the best can remain.

ᕯ *Prayer* ᕬ

Father God, I pray that out of Your glorious riches You may strengthen me with power through Your Spirit in my inner being, so that You, Christ Jesus, may dwell in my heart through faith and that I may be one with You and remain in You. And I pray that I will be rooted and established in love and may have power, together with all the saints, to grasp how wide and long and high and deep Your love for me is, Jesus, and to know this love that surpasses knowledge—that I may be filled to the measure of all Your fullness. You are able to do immeasurably more than all I ask or imagine, according to Your power that is at work within me. To You be glory in the church and in Christ Jesus throughout all generations, forever and ever! Amen.

—Ephesians 3:16-21

ᕯ *Practicing the Spiritual Life* ᕬ

1. Do you ever fear surrendering your will and releasing your life to God? Why—or why not? What truths in this chapter encourage you to release any fear or to stand strong in your fearless trust?

2. As you read this chapter, did you recognize a need to release to God a particular area of your life? If so, what was it?

3. Describe a time when God asked you to serve in an area where you felt unqualified. What happened? What lessons, if any, did you learn?

4. As you think about a difficult relationship or situation in your life right now, what would it look like to believe that, as Corrie ten Boom wrote, "when Jesus is with you, the worst can happen and the best remains"?

Part Five

THE

SERVANT

LIFE

CHAPTER 19

PRESENT YOURSELF FOR SERVICE

I know your deeds, your love and faith,
your service and perseverance,
and that you are now doing
more than you did at first.

—*Revelation 2:19*

Throughout my fifty-eight years of being a Christian, God has taught me many things, but two lessons stand out to me because they changed not only my understanding of God but also the course of my life and my service for Him.

First, I have learned that God calls all Christians to serve Him daily throughout our life according to *His* plans, not our own. I cannot think of one person in the Bible who volunteered to serve God. The Lord chose men and women to follow Him, and He showed up unexpectedly in their lives and asked them to do certain things for Him.

He clearly called the boy Samuel to be a priest; David, to be king; Isaiah, to be a prophet; and Abraham, to be the father of the Israelites. God called these people to serve Him in ways they never would have chosen to serve or imagine themselves serving. Likewise, God has plans for us that we would never choose or imagine.

Second, God is sovereign. Recognizing that truth compels us to live a God-driven, God-centered life, not a me-centered life. Pastors, missionaries, and ministry staff are not the only ones called to full-time service for God. Again, the truth is that every believer is to serve God and minister to others, each and every day, according to His will. Surrendering to God's plans for us is necessary if we are to be women of God.

OUT OF THE ORDINARY

Serving God begins with the smallest, most ordinary tasks. It's in our daily work, whatever that work is, and through our ordinary actions and words that we can all minister to others. In fact, how we yield to the sovereign God's desires in the smallest of tasks matters a lot to Him.

When we're seeking His guidance and obeying Him, every mundane duty, every big job or small job, everything we do at any given moment of our day can be a sacred act of service to the King of kings.

Thomas Merton made this observation: "The requirements of a work to be done can be understood as the will of God. If I am supposed to hoe a garden or make a table, then I will be obeying God if I am true to the task I am performing. To do the work carefully and well, with love and respect for the nature of my task and with due attention to its purposes, is to unite myself to God's will in my work."[62]

God is more concerned about what we do at this moment than what we do tomorrow. If we keep doing what God wants us to do now, we'll accomplish all that He desires us to accomplish during our lifetime.

Other believers echo that thought: "[Jesus] is both the Way itself and the One who walks beside us on that Way, bearing on His shoulders the responsibility for our affairs. We can go shopping with Jesus, go to work with Him, do the most menial tasks in the house with Him, and undertake the largest responsibilities in our profession with Him. If we are cleansed from our sin as we go, we shall many times a day turn to Him to seek His guidance, to ask His help, or just to praise Him for His love and sufficiency."[63]

Present-moment service of our Lord requires a constant awareness of what we're doing right now: *Who does God want me to help or speak to now? What hard or easy task can I do for His glory?* Present-moment service doesn't replace a more formal ministry we're already doing.

Present-moment service simply means that we remain open to unforeseen opportunities to share the Lord—the truth about Him and His love—throughout the day. Growing to know God better means being more attuned to His Spirit guiding us to serve.[64]

Elisabeth Elliot agreed that taking up our cross and following Jesus means serving God right where we are: "What is the cross? It is, I believe, the thing required of me today. 'Let him take up his cross daily,' Jesus said, 'and follow me.' Some duty lies on my doorstep right now. It may be a simple thing that I have known for a long time I ought to do, but it has been easy to avoid. It is probably the thing that springs to my mind when I pray. . . . It may be that although I have been doing something I ought to do, I have never done it without grudging. The so-called 'cross' which I could not avoid I may, for a change, take up with gladness. Might I not then, for the first time, be on the way to true discipleship?"[65]

DISCOVERING GOD'S GUIDANCE

Again, serving God in our daily work does not negate a call to a specific place of ministry. How do we know the ways God wants us to serve Him in the day to day? And how do we know what ministry God wants us involved in? And what if we make the wrong choice? God is more than willing to guide us when we genuinely desire to know His will, and He uses divine appointments, Bible passages, books, people, and circumstances to show us His will.

How and where, with whom and to whom the Lord calls us to minister daily, is as individual and unique as we are. Furthermore, God has many purposes for each ministry we do and for each trial we go through.

For example, Herb was a friend of ours who had AIDS. The Lord transformed him, redeemed his life, and, before he died, gave him a ministry to others with AIDS and to their families. Because Herb was open to sharing God's grace in his life, many people committed their lives to Christ, renewed their faith, were ministered to as they were dying, and gained the courage they needed to face illness and loss.

When we are open and sensitive to the leading of the Holy Spirit, He shows us many surprising ways He can use even a single experience from our life. God wants us to know His plans for us. In fact, "the word *will* as in 'God's will' comes from a Greek word that carries feeling and even passion.

When we say 'What is God's will?' we are asking, 'What is God's deep, heartfelt desire for our lives and our world? What does this God who loves us want for us above all? What is God committed to accomplishing on our behalf no matter what the cost?'"[66]

We can ask these same questions of our own life as it unfolds: What is God's deep, heartfelt desire for my life, for how I am to use the talents, time, and treasure He has given me? What does this loving God most want me to do for Him?

Circumstances are one way God guides our steps in answer to these questions. Ron's and my decision to move from Orange County, for example, was motivated by our circumstances: our home was in an unsafe neighborhood. Common sense and the doctor as well told us that Ron needed to get out of his high-stress job. He did far better when he worked under less pressure and did not have to travel long distances on congested freeways.

The Lord may also impress *certain desires upon our hearts* in order to guide our steps. This may be the most confusing means He chooses since it is difficult to distinguish between our own ideas and the Holy Spirit's urgings. Ron and I both wanted to move to Santa Maria, and the desire grew stronger and stronger over time. But we weren't sure if the desire was rooted in our own desperation or if God was leading us.

Then three friends who have no relationship with one another each told us that they felt strongly that God was going to move us to Santa Maria. Still, it wasn't until we had lived here for more than a year that I was certain it was God's will for us. Since then, the Lord has confirmed in numerous different ways that we came here by His guiding hand, especially when Ron suddenly went blind and we were living near our adult children.

God may use *other people* to confirm His place of service for us. Elisabeth Elliot talked about the importance of seeking guidance: "we ought to look first of all to those with whom we have some special relationship . . . God works always with perfect wisdom, always with perfect love, and nearly always in conjunction with human means."[67] The Bible tells us, "Where no counsel is, the people fall: but in the multitude of counselors there is safety" (Proverbs 11:14 KJV).

We don't see ourselves as others see us; we're often blind to our strengths and weaknesses, to our gifts and a lack of giftedness. Sadly, many believers have served in volunteer church activities or even full-time ministries when they were totally unsuited for the job. They dogmatically held on to what they thought was the call of God for their life when it was obvious to those who knew them that they didn't belong in the position where they were serving. We need the counsel and wisdom of others to determine what God would have us do to serve Him.

We also need to remember that though we may feel the strong leading of the Lord, our feelings are not always an accurate gauge of God's will. Enjoying certain ministries doesn't mean we are called to do them or suited for the task. On the other hand, we may not enjoy certain avenues of service, and that's exactly where we belong.

God has called me numerous times to serve Him in ways I never would have chosen for myself. Unknowingly agreeing with God, people who believed I had a gift in certain areas have led me to be involved in ministries I would never have imagined doing. On the other hand, God has soundly shut the door for me to serve in ministries when I had a great desire to do exactly that. Now as I look back over the years, I see that God's choices were the wisest ones.

Again, God wants us to get to know Him better and better so that His will becomes ours. Oswald Chambers put it this way: "Our Lord never dictated to His Father, and we are not here to dictate to God; we are here to submit to His will so that He may work through us what He wants. When we realize this, He will make us broken bread and poured-out wine to feed and nourish others."[68]

KNOWING GOD'S WILL FOR US

Many of us wish God would write us a personal letter or fly a banner across the sky with clear directions. As we seek to discern how God wants us to serve, it helps to look at what we already know. For example, God calls us to serve Him by giving generously to those in need. In our you-can-have-it-all materialistic society, it's extremely difficult to overcome the compulsion to acquire more, but maintaining our possessions can become an all-consuming task. If only we could learn "to enjoy things without owning them"[69]—or without having them own us!

We also know that God calls us to serve Him according to His time frame, not our own. Elisabeth Elliot shared this confession: "I realize that nearly all of my trouble with finding out the will of God came because I wanted it too soon. . . . My acceptance of his timing was a rigorous exercise in trust. . . . I would always ask desperately to be shown God's will, but he never showed it to me until the time came. And when it came, it was as clear as the sunlight."[70]

We may encounter disappointments when we serve the Lord, because we had our mind set on how a particular ministry should turn out. We may spend hours planning and preparing for a ministry event, but one key person doesn't follow through and everything falls apart. Our expectations of what God should do and how people should respond result in our disillusionment. That's why many Christians give up on ministry, feel burned out, and refuse to serve again.

But if we let go of our expectations and change our focus from results that we want to whom we can minister to and why we minister, we'll have the joy of seeing God work. Our loving obedience glorifies God even though the outcome may be disappointing or far different from what we had expected.

Also, if the person we've devoted many hours ministering to doesn't choose to follow Christ or turns away from Him, we need to trust that God is working in other ways. When we consider the ministries of Jesus, the disciples, and the apostle Paul, we see that many of the people they encountered didn't believe Jesus was the Messiah or choose to follow Him. Similarly, those we serve may fail to be committed to the Savior, but He always remains faithful.

God asks us to seek His guidance and then serve Him according to His plans, not our own—and, as Elisabeth Elliot learned, to do what He says: "It is not reasonable to ask for guidance in one matter if we are aware that in another matter we have rejected the guidance already given. Let us first go back, if possible, to where we turned away. If this is no longer possible, let us confess our sin."[71]

The hardest place of service, the one that tests our obedience the most, is doing what we don't want to do even though the Lord has made it clear to us that we should. And if we serve in that capacity with a bitter, begrudging attitude, we'll do harm to the name of Christ and hurt others in the process. This is when we need to rely on God's strength, surrender to Him, and do His will with open hands and loving heart.

If we end up facing trials and hard times when we thought we'd stepped out in response to God's leading, we may wonder if we missed His direction.

But over the years I have come to realize that heartaches and difficulties are not an indicator that I am out of the Lord's will. In fact, many times trials have become more intense when I was doing exactly what God wanted.

Every time I write a book, for example, hindrances spring up worse than weeds. During this particular writing time, our clothes dryer broke, the spout on our kitchen faucet came off and a geyser of water started to flood our kitchen, and our dishwasher died of old age and went to the dump. The toilets plugged up.

My husband's blindness and confusion has worsened; our son is critically ill with auto-immune deficiency diseases; and I've had chronic infections. The intensity of the illnesses and the household things that keep going wrong are overwhelming.

We take care of our three granddaughters, and we enjoy them greatly; they still need my time and attention and so does my messy house. But I have critical deadlines to meet and can't keep up with it all.

I sometimes laugh when one more thing goes wrong because I realize that the enemy of my soul will do all he can to prevent completion of *A Woman's Heart for God*. The Lord has sustained me in the midst of all this chaos that hinders my concentration.

Ron and my dear prayer warrior friends have held me up before the Lord during this time. This past Sunday, during a particularly stressful time, a pastor friend called right in the middle of a crisis and prayed with me.

I often wonder why. It seems as if God is allowing all of these trials to work against what He wants me to accomplish. What He teaches me over and again is to humble myself before Him, to submit myself to the guidance of my editors and their revisions, and to let go and let Him take over. The Lord alone has accomplished through me what He desired, and I cannot take any credit at all. Because I know in these intense trials, I was powerless to finish this project on my own; the support of God and others brought me through it. When we are powerless, God is most glorified.

This is what it means to deny ourselves for the sake of Christ: we stop looking inward, concerned only about ourselves. We start looking outward, watching for what the Lord wants us to do for His sake.

LEARNING TO ACCEPT GOD'S PLANS

As I've already mentioned, God's place of service for us may not be the place we would choose, but it *is* the place that will ultimately bring us joy.

Many years ago when I was working for a ministry as a book editor, I thought I would be serving there for the rest of my working years. When the ministry announced it was moving out of state, my heart's desire was to move with the ministry. But I did not feel a peace about that possibility for my family and me. I kept wavering about the decision.

While we were on a brief family vacation and then during the first days after we returned home, the Lord showed me that He would guide me to new places of service. When I spent several hours reading the Word, verse after verse was about how God loves, comforts, and guides His people as a shepherd guides his sheep.

By divine coincidence the weekly hymn in my devotional book included the words I needed: "Savior, like a shepherd lead us, / Much we need thy tender care; / In thy pleasant pastures feed us, / For our use thy folds prepare.... / We are thine, thou dost befriend us, / be the guardian of our way.... / Thou hast loved us, love us still."

On Sunday morning when we went to church, I was astounded when the usher handed me the worship service bulletin. The theme for the morning service was "The Lord Is My Shepherd." The hymns were "All the Way My Savior Leads Me," "He Leadeth Me," and "Savior, Like a Shepherd Lead Us." The title of the message was "It's Okay to Be a Sheep When You Have a Good Shepherd."

One of the verses read during worship was "In your unfailing love you will lead the people you have redeemed" (Exodus 15:13). I cried openly during that service: I was so moved by the Lord's outpouring of love to me and by His promise that He would care for and guide me.

The following Monday morning before work, I noticed that my readings and several different verses were about God's love. The hymn for the week in my devotions was "Love Divine, All Loves Excelling," and it included the line "Breathe, O breathe thy loving Spirit / Into every troubled breast."

Tuesday morning when I arose to have my devotions, I wondered what message the Lord would send me off to work with today. I'd awakened at 3:30 a.m. due to a sleep disorder and stress. The Lord reminded me to rejoice in those sufferings, because they produce perseverance, character, and hope—and "hope does not disappoint us, because God has poured out his love into our hearts" (Romans 5:5).

My verse cards also challenged me to love the Lord my God with all my heart, soul, and strength (Deuteronomy 6:5). Then I read the same promise in two different verses: God will instruct me, teach me the way to go, counsel and watch over me, guide me continually, and satisfy my soul in drought (Psalm 32:8; Isaiah 58:11).

I wrote in my journal: "It has been a long season of drought without adequate watering of my soul and spirit. The Lord poured out His promises of guidance and love when I felt depressed and hopeless about my future, about giving up working with people I dearly love, about leaving work that I enjoy more than any other I have done before."

God had spoken to my heart in the depths of my grief, and I began to feel a new sense of adventure as I waited to see what the Lord had planned for me. I felt humbled and grateful for how He had ministered to me and met my innermost needs with His outpouring of tender promises. For seven days God comforted me with assurance of His love and guidance.

So Ron and I decided not to make the move out of state. Before my final day at the ministry, God graciously provided me with an excellent part-time teaching position at the college where I'd been an instructor before. Since then, due to many unexpected health problems and trials, I've realized that the choice God made for my life was the wisest one. God had known what was ahead of me, and of course His gracious, loving choice proved best for me as well as for my family.

And God continued to assure me of His care. I was deeply touched six months later when, at the ministry's last chapel, we sang the hymn "All the Way My Savior Leads Me": "Can I doubt His tender mercy,

/ Who through life has been my Guide? / Heav'nly peace, divinest comfort, / Here by faith in Him to dwell!/For I know, whate'er befall me, / Jesus doeth all things well; . . . / All the way my Savior leads me; / O the fullness of His love!"

⌣

Even after we earnestly pray, read the Word, and seek the Lord's direction and godly counsel, our decision is nevertheless a step of faith. Once we make a decision and take that step, we may gain spiritual insight or a greater understanding of a situation and therefore need to adjust our course. Changing your mind like that is not a sign of failure; in fact, it may actually be a sign of spiritual wisdom and sensitivity to the Holy Spirit's guidance.

Finally, as we look for opportunities to serve the Lord, the most important thing is for us to be open to God's leading. He longs for us to present ourselves to Him as women eager to know Him better and serve Him faithfully.

⌣ *Prayer* ⌣

Lord, prepare me for works of service, so that the body of Christ may be built up. . . . Teach me how to be as those who are wise and understanding. Help me to show it by my good life, by deeds done in the humility that comes from wisdom . . . Help me to be ready to do whatever is good, to slander no one, to be peaceable and considerate, and to show true humility toward all people . . . Teach me how to use the gifts You have given me to serve others, faithfully administering Your grace in many different ways. When I speak, may I do so as one speaking the very words of God. When I serve, may I do it with the strength You provide, so that in all things You may be praised through Jesus Christ . . . Bless my eyes that I may see and my ears that I may hear. . . . May Your Word be sown in the good soil of my heart, because I hear and understand it. . . . As I serve You, may my life produce a crop, yielding a hundred, sixty, or thirty times what was sown. . . . Above all, help me to love others deeply, because love covers a multitude of sins.

—Ephesians 4:12; James 3:13; Titus 3:1–2; 1 Peter 4:10–11; Matthew 13:16, 23; 1 Peter 4:8

✎ *Practicing the Spiritual Life* ✎

1. When, if ever, have you questioned God's guidance? When, if ever, have you taken a step of faith, encountered trials, and then doubted your ability to know His will? Explain.

2. Describe a time when you served God in a place you did not choose, but a place that ultimately brought you great joy.

3. Jesus showed us with His words and His actions that we serve Him best when we do so with a servant's attitude, however menial a task is. Write down a task you can do with a servant's heart to minister to a specific person. Set a date and time to serve in that way.

4. What do you see as the connection between serving God and believing God is sovereign?

CHAPTER 20

GIVE THE GIFT OF GRACE

*Each one should use whatever gift he has received
to serve others, faithfully administering
God's grace in its various forms.*

—*1 Peter 4:10*

Years ago I taught English in southern California to immigrants from many parts of the world. Most students had families to care for and worked at minimum wage or below in water-bottling factories and other backbreaking jobs. Many of them lived with their families in a single rented room, sharing a communal kitchen and bathroom with other families. One man attended class all week even though he was living in his car with his wife, an infant, and two preschool daughters. The students told me about their lives, but they weren't complaining as they did so. They spoke about their desire to learn English quickly and to work hard in order to make a better life for themselves and their children. Their diligence, despite their difficult lives, amazed me.

ACTS OF KINDNESS

Kenn was one of my students. Learning English was extremely hard for him because he was illiterate in his own language. He always sat in a front seat, but I had a large class and was unable to give him much individual help. I asked more advanced students to assist Kenn, but his ability to learn seemed limited. He didn't speak often, but when he did, most of us had difficulty understanding him.

At the end of the semester, Kenn brought me an appreciation gift: a pair of black patent leather shoes, with bows, in my exact size. I have no idea how he knew what size to buy. I wore the shoes at our closing class party. When I pointed to them and thanked Kenn, he didn't say a word, but he did giggle with delight and embarrassment. I felt that I had not merited such a gift. Out of that class of students, I had helped him least.

A couple of years later I received another unexpected gift. I was teaching my class when a secretary came to tell me that my father had passed away. I quickly excused the students and left campus. On the day of the funeral, my family and I arrived a few minutes before the service began. Some of my Vietnamese students, dressed in black, were standing in the lobby. They had arrived half an hour before and had been waiting for me. Each student shook my hand, offered sympathy, and then quietly left before the service started.

When I entered the funeral chapel, I discovered an enormous floral wreath. Two purple ribbons were draped across the front with these words of condolence handwritten in silver: "With deeper sympathy—Vietnamese Students." This expression of love surprised and humbled me.

I've found that some of the poorest and most unpretentious people minister to me the most. I will, for instance, always remember a young man in one of my vocational classes. He was a migrant farmworker who worked backbreaking hours. He had a sleeping bag for a bed, an old car, and few other possessions, yet he constantly helped other students. I don't speak Spanish, so he translated for them and helped them with their textbook assignments. He didn't help in any official capacity; he simply gave himself to others wherever he saw a need.

The generosity of these students reminds me of the story Jesus told about the poor widow who put two copper coins into the temple treasury. He told the people around Him, "All these people gave their gifts out of their wealth; but she out of her poverty put in all she had to live on" (Luke 21:4). Some of the poorest people on this earth are the most gracious and generous. What touched my heart in the situations I just described was not the cost of the gifts, but what those gifts cost the givers.

These acts of kindness are a picture of what God gave me by His grace at such a great sacrifice—the death of His only Son as payment for my sins. Just as I could not give a material gift of equal value to thank my students, I cannot give Christ a gift of equal value to thank Him. He bestowed His favor upon me even though I did not merit it.

The kindest thing—the only thing—I could do for my students was to express my deep gratitude to each of them and continue to serve them as their teacher. In the same way, having received Jesus's gift of grace and sacrificial kindness to me, I can only express my deep gratitude to Him with heartfelt thanksgiving and then commit to serve Him with my life. Put simply, I can respond to God's grace by giving grace to others.

COMPASSIONATE GRACE

When Ron and I moved to Santa Maria, I continued teaching English. Most of the immigrants who attended my classes worked in the local strawberry fields. In the intense heat of the sun or in the pouring rain, these workers would stoop over rows of berries handpicking that ripe, luscious fruit we enjoy without thought.

If you've ever tramped through a muddy field with your shoes sinking into the mire, you know how exhausting just a short walk can be. Imagine stooping all day long, slogging through the mud, coming home after ten or more hours of bone-wearying labor, showering, eating, and then going to class because you want to make a better life for yourself.

During one class, the students asked if we could discuss discrimination. I asked them to write their discussion questions on cards. One asked, "Why don't the field workers receive the best salary if the people who work in the fields work more than office workers?"

I couldn't answer that question, and I couldn't improve their situation. But I could love them as God had called me to love them: I could teach them, encourage them, and respect them. At one time I had been blind to their needs, but God opened my heart and then gave me the privilege of serving them.

Hear what the Lord Himself said about King Josiah of the Old Testament: "'He defended the cause of the poor and needy, and so all went well. Is that not what it means to know me?' declares the Lord" (Jeremiah 22:16). Do you see that important truth? God equates helping the poor and needy with knowing Him.

Having a heart for God means showing compassion to all people, not just those who meet our standard of acceptability. "This is what the Lord Almighty says: 'Administer true justice; show mercy and compassion to one another. Do not oppress the widow or the fatherless, the alien or the poor. In your hearts do not think evil of each other'" (Zechariah 7:9-10).

A woman I once knew was a humble, unpretentious person who had led a very hard life. She'd had polio as a child and suffered crippling pain from the disease as an adult. But she was a great woman of prayer. When she interceded for others, God answered. She also had an uncanny sense of when others needed prayer, and she would call them.

When my husband Ron had heart surgery, she prayed that God would send many people to be with me and comfort me during the operation. It wasn't until I told her how amazed I was that seventeen people had waited with me the day of the surgery that she told me what she had prayed for us.

Often the most humble people, those who won't be found on the society page of the newspaper, are the best givers of grace. If they are needy, perhaps financially or physically, they will nevertheless minister to those around them who are emotionally or spiritually needy. When we recognize our own neediness, we can not only receive God's grace but also share that grace when and where He calls us.

SACRIFICIAL GRACE

Having a heart for God also means extending grace in tangible ways as well. Paul commended the Macedonian churches for their giving: "Out of the most severe trial, their overflowing joy and their extreme poverty welled up in rich generosity. For I testify that they gave as much as they were able, and even beyond their ability" (2 Corinthians 8:2-3). Then Paul urged the Corinthians to follow the same example: "Just as you excel in everything—in faith, in speech, in knowledge, in complete earnestness and in your love for us—see that you also excel in this grace of giving" (2 Corinthians 8:7).

My husband's parents offer a beautiful example of sacrificial giving. They had a small home and a below-average income, but if they learned about the needs of a single mother, a widow, the unemployed, or the poor, they gave clothes, food, and money. They tithed faithfully to their church and sent offerings to missionaries. They gave far more than they could afford, but they never went without.

When my mother-in-law, who had Alzheimer's disease, went into a convalescent home, her friend Marion visited her faithfully. We lived fifteen hundred miles away, so Marion advised us of my mother-in-law's needs the entire eight years she was in the home. Ron's parents had helped Marion when she was widowed, and she remembered their kindness. By God's tender grace, my mother-in-law was cared for in the same way she had cared for others.

Helping others in practical ways like these encourages them in their faith. Ron used to take clothes to a Christian rehabilitation home for former prisoners, and I know that prison chaplains always need Bibles and Christian literature for the inmates. In addition to faithful financial support, missionaries often need cars, clothing, furnishings, and help in finding housing when they come home on furlough.

Give children's clothing and furniture to young families in your church. Or gather several people and spend a few hours making meals, cleaning house, and doing laundry for someone who is seriously ill. My friend Doris adopts women in convalescent homes, visits them regularly, takes them teddy bears and other small gifts, and regularly prays for and with them.

Prayer is one of the most vital ways we can meet people's needs, and it should not be underestimated. But at the same time, saying, "I will pray for you" may just be an excuse for not showing kindness in a tangible way.

⌒

Jesus showed us how we are to follow His gracious, humble ways. A caring servant to the hungry, helpless, needy, and poor, Jesus gave us an example to follow.

When He returns, our inheritance will be based on what we do for those among us who are in the greatest need.

When we feed the hungry, we are feeding Christ. When we give water to the thirsty, we are giving our Savior a drink. When we invite strangers into our churches and homes, we are inviting Christ. When we give clothes to those who need them, we are clothing our Lord; when we care for the sick, we are caring for Him; when we visit those in prison, we are visiting Him (Matthew 25:34-40). When we do acts like these with loving-kindness, we are giving and living grace.

⌒ *Prayer* ⌒

Lord, teach me how to use whatever gift I have received to serve others, faithfully administering Your grace in its various forms. . . . Then I will do good deeds, as one who has brought up children, who has practiced hospitality to strangers, who has washed the feet of the saints, who has helped to relieve the distressed, and devoted myself to doing good in every way. . . . I will also consider how I may spur others on toward love and good deeds. . . . I will let my light so shine before others that they may see my good works and glorify You, Father, who are in heaven. . . . Lord, I have freely received; therefore, I will freely give. . . . I will open my hands to the poor; yes, I will reach out to the needy with my hands filled. . . . Then I will know the blessing of generously sharing my food with the poor. . . . By being generous, my soul will prosper and be enriched. When I refresh others, I will myself be refreshed.

—1 PETER 4:10; 1 TIMOTHY 5:10 AMP; HEBREWS 10:24; MATTHEW 5:16
KJV; MATTHEW 10:8; PROVERBS 31:20 AMP; PROVERBS 22:9; 11:25

⮿ *Practicing the Spiritual Life* ⮾

1. When have you received God's grace through another person? Be specific.

2. Why does God want us to show grace and mercy to others, to believers and nonbelievers alike?

3. Ask the Lord to show you someone with a specific need and how you can meet that need in a compassionate, sensitive, and caring way. Make a commitment to yourself and even to God to do that act of kindness by a certain time.

4. When have you found that giving to others also brings you joy? What does this reality say about the character of God?

CHAPTER 21

REJOICE IN THE LORD ALWAYS

Glory in his holy name;
let the hearts of those who
seek the LORD rejoice.

—*1 Chronicles 16:10*

The sun, pure and radiant, cast a fiery glow across the crystal-blue sky. Clouds in patches of apricot, rose, and gray shone like satin. In places, vivid white light broke through. Below, the Pacific Ocean was a sea of glass. But it was the crown of the sun that transfixed me. Luminous beams fanning out into the sky seemed to touch the edge of heaven. I was glimpsing God's glory.

That iridescent crown of light reminded me of the apostle John's vision recorded in Revelation: "I saw what looked like a sea of glass mixed with fire and, standing beside the sea, those who had been victorious over the beast and his image and over the number of his name. They held harps given them by God and sang the song of Moses the servant of God and the song of the Lamb: 'Great and marvelous are your deeds, Lord God Almighty. Just and true are your ways, King of the ages. Who will not fear you, O Lord, and bring glory to your name? For you alone are holy'" (Revelation 15:2-4).

Seeing the crown of sunlight left me awestruck. As I drove up Highway 101, I looked for a place to pull over. When I finally found a spot, the golden crown had slipped behind the distant islands. Even as I spent a few minutes worshiping God and watching the waning sunset, the concerns of my heart weighed me down.

Rejoicing in the Lord—even as I watched a gorgeous sunset—is the weakest area of my spiritual life. I spend only seconds rejoicing compared to the hours I spend praying for personal needs.

I imagine that may be true for you as well. We spend a lot of time praying for ourselves and our loved ones, and God does want us to take those needs to Him. But He also wants us to rejoice in Him, to remember that He is greater than any earthly need we may have.

So I want to end this book with a call to praise because I have found praise to be so important in my own spiritual life—important to developing a devotional life, to prayer, to enduring intense testing, to following God's call to be a servant, and to knowing better the Lover of my soul.

STANDING IN GOD'S HOLY PRESENCE

What a day it will be when we join that vast heavenly chorus of Christians in songs of praise. Purified at last from all our sins, we will find our joy in the risen and reigning Lord heightened by the trials through which we have passed. How magnificent it will be one day to join with God's victorious saints singing to the glory of their God triumphant! What indescribable joy as we worship our glorious Savior!

I long for that day, even as I wonder why worshiping and praising God is such a struggle for me now. I am sometimes reluctant to worship God because when I do, my own unworthiness, my feelings of guilt and shame, and my mental battle with evil thoughts overwhelm me. So I withdraw instead of dealing with the feelings and sins that keep me from being drawn into the presence of a holy God, who seems to ask far more of me than I can ever be.[72]

Jack Hayford offered this insight: "From one standpoint, you are exactly right if you feel that you're too sinful to stand in the presence of God and worship. But let our worship 'in Christ' in 'the beauty of His holiness' remind us how His cleansing blood has touched us. Not only our tongues but our whole being 'washed in the blood of the lamb'! It is overwhelming to reflect on our sinfulness before a sinless God, but let us recognize with equal impact that through Christ we have been cleansed, enabled through no righteousness of our own, to stand before the holy God."[73]

Yet keeping me from having a heart of gratitude are my pride, my grief over unanswered prayers, my dissatisfaction with an answer when it does come, and my way of always wanting more from God. I'm quick to beg and slow to praise. But God wants us to praise Him for who He is, not for what He will do for us. Pure praise is free of pride and expectation. Therefore pure praise, offered by a humble heart, encourages others in their faith and gives them hope that God is more than able to meet their greatest needs.

So the questions we need to ask are *Why do we worship God?* and *How do we praise Him?*

Once we know how to worship God, may we exalt Him with lips that sing hymns and songs of praise, with hearts that rejoice in Him, and with lives that glorify His name.

WORSHIP THE LORD

Hear the psalmist call people to worship: "Come, let us bow down in worship, let us kneel before the LORD our Maker" (Psalm 95:6). The intertwining of worshiping God and knowing God is a beautiful mystery: as we worship the Lord, we get to know Him better, and as we know Him better, we worship Him more wholeheartedly.

A. W. Tozer wrote this: "Acquaint thyself with God . . . To know God is at once the easiest and most difficult thing in the world. It is easy because the knowledge is not won by hard mental toil, but is something freely given. As sunlight falls free on the open field, so the knowledge of the holy God is a free gift to men who are open to receive it." [74]

One way to know God better is to meditate on the names of God, for they reveal His nature, His promises, and His personal relationship with us. So exalt Almighty God, for none is mightier than He. Extol the Maker of heaven and earth, for He created and governs the vast galaxies of the universe. Hail the Alpha and Omega, the First and Last. Magnify the Everlasting Father who reigns on high.

Be thankful to the Shepherd and Overseer of our souls for watching over us. Love Jesus with the adoration of a little child. Honor the Crucified One for dying for our sins. So join me in giving glory to our Blessed Redeemer, who is our one and only Savior.

Express gratitude to the God of grace and mercy, who delivers us from evil. Offer sacrifices of thanksgiving to the Holy Comforter, Consoler, and Counselor, who bears our sorrows and hears our every cry. Bow down before the great I AM WHO I AM. Praise the King of kings and Lord of lords. Sing to the Bright Morning Star, Master of everything, Rock of all ages. Shout for joy to our wonderful Lord. Worship Father, Son, and Holy Spirit. Sing hallelujah to Jesus Christ, the Lamb!

PRAISE IS A SACRIFICE

"Through Jesus, therefore, let us continually offer to God a sacrifice of praise—the fruit of lips that confess his name" (Hebrews 13:15). Be thankful that the Lord knows and cares that our praises are often a sacrifice. We may grieve over heartaches at the same time that we are expressing gratitude for God's presence and provision.

God never expects us to praise Him for the evil, injustice, or wrongdoing that afflicts us. What He desires from us is a sacrifice of thanksgiving for His loving presence and His guiding hand that leads us through these trials. He knows our losses, and He wants to comfort and be with us in the valley of sorrow.

Do we not feel the hurts of those we love more deeply than those of strangers? God feels even more keenly the pain of those who are His, who are His very own beloved ones. He knows the grief of suffering, "but," He adds, "rejoice that you participate in the sufferings of Christ, so that you may be overjoyed when his glory is revealed" (1 Peter 4:13).

When we accuse God of abandoning us, we separate ourselves from His ever-caring presence. But when we thank the Lord sacrificially, no matter how insincere we may feel, He lifts us up and fills our hearts with peace and joy that will sustain us. Praise Him for His love. Praise Him that He sees our afflictions and knows the anguish of our soul (Psalm 31:7). Thank Him that He alone is our refuge (Psalm 64:10).

"Praise the Lord. Do it again; continue to do it; do it better and more heartily; do it in growing numbers; do it at once. There are good reasons for praising the Lord, and among the first is this—for the Lord is good. He is so good that there is none good in the same sense or degree. He is so good that all good is found in him, flows from him, and is rewarded by him." [75]

SING TO THE LORD

"Sing to the LORD, you saints of his; praise his holy name" (Psalm 30:4). Singing hymns lifts our hearts into the very presence of God and causes us to at least momentarily forget ourselves. Some would even say that song is the highest and most sacred means of worshiping God. Song thrills our hearts, causes us to weep with joy, and fills our soul with the glory of God.

Expressing "praise by sacred song is one of our greatest delights. We were created for this purpose, and hence it is a joy to us. It is a charming duty to praise the lovely name of our God. All pleasure is to be found in the joyful worship of Jehovah; all joys are in his sacred name, as perfumes lie slumbering in a garden of flowers. The mind expands, the soul is lifted up, the heart warms, the whole being is filled with delight when we are engaged in singing the high praises of our Father, Redeemer, Comforter." [76]

REMEMBER THE PAST

"I will remember the deeds of the LORD; yes, I will remember your miracles of long ago" (Psalm 77:11). Acknowledging God's presence with us in the past is another way to praise Him. As Spurgeon observed, "Gratitude for one mercy refreshes the memory as to thousands of others. One silver link in the chain draws up a long series of tender remembrances. Here is eternal work for us, for there can be no end to the showing forth of all his deeds of love."[77]

REJOICE IN THE LORD

Just as the sunset on the Pacific Ocean once reminded me of God's glory, years before that a sunrise moved me to worship. Throughout the night, rains had flooded the earth. At daybreak the sun was a round globe of bright-white light, its brilliance so blinding I could only look upon it a few seconds. Beams of light radiating from around the sun streamed through overcast clouds.

With the wonder of a child, I watched the gray clouds, tinged in cotton-white, float across the pure blue sky. The sun cast a soft white glow on the water-laden earth. Glistening drops of water, crystal-clear as Christmas lights, dangled from the branch tips of the sequoia pine in our backyard.

My focus lifted beyond the confines of this earth to the highest heavens, to God who orchestrates radiant white sunrises and glorious fiery sunsets. Yes, I praised Him!

But rejoicing is not merely a feel-good suggestion. It is a command: "Rejoice in the Lord always. I will say it again: Rejoice!" (Philippians 4:4). Rejoice in the Lord constantly, daily, always, and forevermore. We are to join the universe in rejoicing that Christians around the world are proclaiming that Jesus is Savior and Lord. "Let the heavens rejoice, let the earth be glad; let them say among the nations, 'The LORD reigns!'" (1 Chronicles 16:31).

Rejoice in the Lord when those who are lost are found and saved, when sinners repent, and because our names are written in heaven (Luke 10:20; 15:4-10). Rejoice that God is God no matter what our circumstances are today.

As Charles Spurgeon wrote, "Joy is the soul of praise. To delight ourselves in God is most truly to extol him. . . . That God is, and that he is such a God, and our God, ours for ever and ever, should wake within us an unceasing and overflowing joy. To rejoice in temporal comforts is dangerous, to rejoice in self is foolish, to rejoice in sin is fatal, but to rejoice in God is heavenly."[78]

So let us "ascribe to the LORD the glory due his name; and then let us worship the LORD in the splendor of his holiness" (Psalm 29:2). Glory belongs to the Lord God alone, not to angels or to any human beings whom this world worships for their beauty and fame. Glory in His holy name. Give God the honor due Him. Glorify God for the magnificence of His beauty and power, of the brightness and splendor of His holiness.

"I will come and proclaim your mighty acts, O Sovereign LORD; I will proclaim your righteousness, yours alone" (Psalm 71:16). Proclaim God's sovereignty, worshiping Him in Spirit and in truth and according to God's Word (John 4:24).

We have eternal glory to look forward to, but even now let us express our gratitude for our Savior's sovereign reign over our lives, for the fact that He knows every intimate detail about us, and for the truth-filled encouragement that His all-powerful love controls everything that touches our lives.

✒ *Prayer* ✒

"From the rising of the sun to the place where it sets, the name of the LORD is to be praised." . . . "The heavens praise your wonders, O LORD, your faithfulness too, in the assembly of the holy ones." . . . "Praise the LORD. Praise the LORD from the heavens, praise him in the heights above." . . . "Praise him, sun and moon, praise him, all you shining stars. Praise him, you highest heavens and you waters above the skies." . . . "Praise the LORD, O my soul. O LORD my God, you are very great; you are clothed with splendor and majesty." . . . "Shout for joy to the LORD, all the earth. Worship the LORD with gladness; come before him with joyful songs. Know that the LORD is God. It is he who made us, and we are his; we are his people, the sheep of his pasture. Enter his gates with thanksgiving and his courts with praise; give thanks to him and praise his name. For the LORD is good and his love endures forever; his faithfulness continues through all generations."

—PSALM 113:3; 89:5; 148:1, 3-4; 104:1; 100:1-5

✒ *Practicing the Spiritual Life* ✒

1. Why is praise important to our spiritual journey?

2. Of the different ways to praise God mentioned in this chapter, which one do you find easiest to incorporate into your life? Why?

3. What is most likely to keep you from praising God? Why do you think that is?

4. What are two or three truths from this book that changed the way you think about God?

5. Spend time praising God and thanking Him for wanting you to have a heart for Him.

NOTES

1. St. Augustine, *The Confessions of St. Augustine*, trans. by John K. Ryan (New York: Doubleday, 1960), 43.

2. *The Westminster Confession of Faith* (Edinburgh: University Press, 1855), 29–31.

3. A. W. Tozer, *The Knowledge of the Holy* (San Francisco: HarperSanFrancisco, 1961), 79.

4. Ibid., 98.

5. Ibid., 105–106.

6. William Evans, *The Great Doctrines of the Bible* (Chicago: Moody, 1912), 40.

7. Tozer, *Knowledge of the Holy*, 51–52.

8. Ibid., 81.

9. C. H. Spurgeon, "Rest, Rest," a sermon delivered on January 8, 1871 at the Metropolitan Tabernacle, London, UK.

10. "Hands Across the Water," *In Focus* 1, no. 2, Wycliffe Bible Translators (April/May 1996), n.p.

11. Charles R. Swindoll, *The Grace Awakening* (Dallas: Word, 1990), 201.

12. Dietrich Bonhoeffer, *The Cost of Discipleship* (New York: Macmillan, 1959), 46.

13. Ibid., 47–48.

14. Swindoll, *Grace Awakening*, 202.

15. Bill Gasser, "The Run," *The Baptist Bulletin*, October 1996, 11.

16. Henri J. M. Nouwen, *Making All Things New: An Invitation to the Spiritual Life* (San Francisco: Harper & Row, 1981), 46–47.

17. Ibid., 47–49.

18. Jan Johnson, *Journeying Through the Days 1995: A Calendar and Journal for Personal Reflections* (Nashville: The Upper Room, 1994), n.p.

19. Rueben P. Job, *Journeying Through the Days 1994: A Calendar and Journal for Personal Reflection* (Nashville: The Upper Room, 1993), n.p.

20. Johnson, *Journeying 1995*, n.p.

21. Ibid., n.p.

22. Charles Stanley, *A Touch of His Peace* (Grand Rapids: Zondervan, 1993), 81.

23. Richard Foster, *Prayer: Finding the Heart's True Home* (San Francisco: HarperOne, 1992), 9.

24. Rosalind Rinker, *Prayer: Conversing with God* (Grand Rapids: Zondervan, 1959, 1986), 23.

25. Foster, *Prayer*, 10.

26. Ibid., 10–11.

27. O. Hallesby, *Prayer*, trans. by Clarence J. Carlsen (Minneapolis, MN: Augsburg, 1931), 16.

28. Henri J. M. Nouwen in the foreword to *The Practice of the Presence of God* by Brother Lawrence (New York: Doubleday, 1977), 9–10.

29. Brother Lawrence, *The Practice of the Presence of God* (New York: Doubleday, 1977), 101.

30. Ibid., 41, 49.

31. Ibid., 40.

32. Ibid., 101, 68.

33. Ibid., 104.

34. Ibid., 101–102.

35. Ibid., 102.

36. Ibid., 103.

37. Dietrich Bonhoeffer, *Discipleship* (Minneapolis, MN: Fortress, 2001), 163.

38. Elton T. Trueblood, *The New Man for Our Time*, quoted in Rueben P. Job and Norman Shawchuck, *A Guide to Prayer for All God's People* (Nashville: The Upper Room, 1990), 250.

39. For more insight into faith becoming real, see Oswald Chambers, *My Utmost for His Highest* (New York: Dodd, Mead & Company, 1935), October 30, 304.

40. John R. Aurelio, *Mosquitoes in Paradise* (New York: Ballantine, 1985), 101.

41. Elizabeth Kubler-Ross, *On Death and Dying* (New York: Macmillan, 1969), 38–137.

42. Chambers, *My Utmost*, June 4, 156.

43. Ibid., June 5, 157.

44. Catherine Marshall, *Beyond Our Selves* (New York: McGraw-Hill, 1961), 87.

45. Ibid., 94.

46. Ibid., 88.

47. Larry Crabb, *Inside Out* (Colorado Springs: NavPress, 1988), 18.

48. Chambers, *My Utmost*, April 4, 95.

49. Marshall, *Beyond Our Selves*, 86.

50. Ibid.

51. Ibid., 94.

52. Corrie ten Boom with Jamie Buckingham, *Tramp for the Lord* (Old Tappan, NJ: Revell, 1974), 11.

53. Ibid., 12.

54. Ibid., 152-153.

55. Corrie ten Boom, *A Tramp Finds a Home* (Old Tappan, NJ: Revell, 1978), 7.

56. Ten Boom, *Tramp for the Lord*, 44.

57. Ibid., 45.

58. Ibid., 33.

59. Ibid., 185-186.

60. Ibid., 78.

61. Chambers, *My Utmost*, June 15, 167.

62. Thomas Merton, *New Seeds of Contemplation*, quoted in Rueben P. Job and Norman Shawchuck, *A Guide to Prayer for All God's People* (Nashville: The Upper Room, 1990), 354.

63. Roy and Revel Hession, *We Would See Jesus* (Fort Washington, PA: Christian Literature Crusade, 1958), 70.

64. For a classic book on serving God in the present, see *The Sacrament of the Present Moment* by Jean-Pierre De Caussade.

65. Elisabeth Elliot, *A Slow and Certain Light: Some Thoughts on the Guidance of God* (Waco: Word, 1973), 50.

66. Stephen D. Bryant, "Letter to a Friend," *Weavings* (May/June 1989), 355.

67. Elliot, *Slow and Certain Light*, 95-96.

68. Chambers, *My Utmost*, May 15, 136.

Notes

69. Richard J. Foster, *Celebration of Discipline: The Path to Spiritual Growth* (San Francisco: Harper & Row, 1978), 80.

70. Elliot, *Slow and Certain Light,* 88–90.

71. Ibid., 52.

72. Jack Hayford, *The Heart of Praise: Daily Ways to Worship the Father with Psalms* (Ventura: Regal, 1992), 22.

73. Ibid., 22–23.

74. Tozer, *Knowledge of the Holy,* 114–115.

75. Charles Spurgeon, *Psalms,* in The Crossway Classic Commentaries, vol. 1, ed. Alister Mc-Grath, J. I. Packer (Wheaton, IL: Crossway Books, 1993), 303–304.

76. Ibid., 304.

77. Ibid., 25.

78. Ibid., 127.

Sheila Cragg is a mentor for the Jerry B. Jenkins Christian Writers Guild and formerly served as an editor for Focus on the Family Publishing. She has published numerous articles in *Reader's Digest*, *Family Weekly*, and other periodicals as well as six books, including the out-of-print devotional Bible studies *A Woman's Walk with God* and *A Woman's Journey Toward Holiness*, as well as a Scripture prayer journal titled *Near to the Heart of God*.

Her *Experiencing Christ* website ministry at http://womanswalk.com and her blog, *One Woman's Heart for God* at http://www.sheilacragg.blogspot.com/, are centered on encouraging people from around the world (62 countries) in their quest to personally experience an intimate relationship with the Lord. This mission statement summarizes her ministry:

Serve One God the Father, Son, and Holy Spirit.
Support Christians in their desire to experience Christ and
    glorify Him.
Share with seekers who desire to know God.

Sheila is also a young-at-heart grandmother, who loves the Lord, her husband, Ron, two sons, five grandchildren, and dear friends. She enjoys sewing and is a ribbon rose artist. She takes care of her three youngest granddaughters, who live three doors away. They love to come to her house to cook, do crafts, hang out, and have sleepovers. She lives in Santa Maria, on the beautiful central coast of California, famous for its wine grape vineyards and fields of strawberries and broccoli.

WORTHY
PUBLISHING

IF YOU ENJOYED THIS BOOK, WILL YOU CONSIDER SHARING THE MESSAGE WITH OTHERS?

- Mention the book in a Facebook post, Twitter update, Pinterest pin, or blog post.

- Recommend this book to those in your small group, book club, workplace, and classes.

- Head over to facebook.com/worthypublishing, "LIKE" the page, and post a comment as to what you enjoyed the most.

- Tweet "I recommend reading #AWoman'sHeartforGod by @sheilacragg // @worthypub"

- Pick up a copy for someone you know who would be challenged and encouraged by this message.

- Write a review on amazon.com or bn.com.

**WORTHY PUBLISHING
FACEBOOK PAGE**

**WORTHY PUBLISHING
WEBSITE**